Joshua Girling Fitch

Thomas and Matthew Arnold and their Influence on English Education

Joshua Girling Fitch

Thomas and Matthew Arnold and their Influence on English Education

ISBN/EAN: 9783337396428

Printed in Europe, USA, Canada, Australia, Japan

Cover: Foto ©Suzi / pixelio.de

More available books at **www.hansebooks.com**

THOMAS AND MATTHEW ARNOLD

AND

THEIR INFLUENCE ON ENGLISH EDUCATION

BY

SIR JOSHUA FITCH, M.A., LL.D.
Formerly Her Majesty's Inspector of Training Colleges

LONDON
WILLIAM HEINEMANN
1897

CONTENTS

CHAPTER I

PAGE

Difficulties of biography — How Stanley's *Life of Arnold* has surmounted them — Chief incidents of Arnold's life — Influences which shaped his character — Ships and warfare — Literary revival — History and politics — School-boy experience — Religious doubts and difficulties — Evidential theology — His intellectual outfit generally 1

CHAPTER II

Residence at Oxford — Arnold's friends and associates — Marriage and settlement at Laleham — Life as a private tutor — Studies and literary work — Aims and aspirations — Appointment to Rugby 15

CHAPTER III

Rugby and its foundation — Characteristics of ancient endowed grammar schools — Illustrations from statutes of Archbishop Grindal and Dean Colet — The theory of classical education — Milton and the Humanists — Example of an entrance examination — Arnold's scheme of instruction — Latin and Greek not useless, even though forgotten in later life — Evils of mechanical routine — Composition exercises — Versification — Objections to it — School-boy artifices for evading it —

Construing — Bowyer of Christ's Hospital — Translation — Grammar and philology means not ends — Socratic questioning — General characteristics of Arnold's methods 25

CHAPTER IV

Language as a discipline contrasted with natural science — Knowledge of physical facts not the only science — History — Relation of Ancient and Modern History — Its claims as a school subject — Training for citizenship — Example of a school exercise — Niebuhr's researches in Roman History — Arnold's own treatment of the regal period of Rome — His love of history infectious — Geography — Thoroughness in teaching — Qualifications of assistants — School organization — Relation of a head master to governing body . . 52

CHAPTER V

Arnold as a disciplinarian — Moral evils in school — Description of their danger — Mr. Welldon's picture of school life — Fagging — Luxury and idleness — Expulsion — Religious lessons — Chapel services — School sermons — Extravagance — Home influence — Mental cultivation a religious duty — A memorable sermon — Religious exercises — Corporate life of a great school — What is Christian education — Clerical schoolmasters — The influence of Arnold's sermons generally — Punishments — Study of individual character — Games and athletics — *Tom Brown's School Days* — Rugby boys at the Universities — Bishop Percival's estimate . 75

CHAPTER VI

Arnold's extra-scholastic interests — Why such interests are necessary for a teacher — Foreign travel — Extracts from diary — Love of Nature — Intercourse with the poor needed by himself and by his pupils — University settlements and mission work in connexion with public schools — Politics — The Reform Bill — The *Englishman's Register* — The society for the diffusion of useful knowledge — Mechanics' Institutes — The London University — Arnold's attitude towards each of these enterprises 110

CHAPTER VII

The Oxford movement — The Hampden controversy — Arnold's relation to the movement — His views as to the condition of the Church of England and of necessary reforms — Dean Church's estimate of Arnold's ecclesiastical position — The Broad Church — Influence of outside interests on the life of the schoolmaster — The ideal teacher — Regius Professorship of Modern History — Arnold's scheme of lectures — Its partial fulfilment — His early death — Conjectures as to what might have been had he lived — Mr. Forster and the Education Act — Testimonies of Dean Boyle and of the *Times* 135

CHAPTER VIII

Matthew Arnold — The materials for his biography — His wishes — The main facts of his life — His letters — His character — His inspectorship — Distaste for official routine — His relations to managers — A school manager's recollections — The office of a School Inspector — Its opportunities of influence — The Revised Code — Arnold's methods of work — Testimony of his assistant 157

CHAPTER IX

Arnold as an officer of the Education Department — His official reports — Inspection and examination — Formative studies — Learning of poetry — Grammar — Latin and French in the primary school — Science teaching and *Naturkunde* — Distrust of pedagogic rules — General aim and scope of an elementary school — The teacher's personal cultivation — Religious instruction — The Bible in the common school — Arnold's attempt at a school reading-book with extracts from Isaiah — The failure of this attempt 176

CHAPTER X

Matthew Arnold's employment in foreign countries — The Newcastle Commission of 1859 — The Schools Inquiry Commission of 1865 — Special report to the Education Department, 1885 — Democracy — Relation of the State to voluntary action in France and in England — Why Germany interested Arnold less than France — Advantages of State action — The religious difficulty in France — Why a purely secular system became inevitable in that country — A French Eton — Comparison with the English Eton — Endowments under French law — Latin and Greek as taught in French Lycées — Entrance scholarships — Leaving examinations — Instruction in civic life and duties 200

CHAPTER XI

Arnold's views of English society — The three classes, the Barbarians, the Philistines, the Populace — Characteristics of the Philistine or middle class — Why his diagnosis, though true in the main, was inadequate — The want of culture among Nonconformists — The disabilities under which they had suffered — A sonnet —

CONTENTS

Illustration of the difference between public schools and private "academies" — Schools for special trades, sects, or professions — Hymns — Effects of his polemic in favour of a system of secondary instruction . . 220

CHAPTER XII

Arnold as a literary critic, a humorist, and as a poet — Criticism and its functions — Comparison with Sainte Beuve — Examples of his critical judgments — Homer, Pope, and Dryden, Byron, Wordsworth, Burke, Tennyson, Charlotte Brontë, and Macaulay — The gift of humour indispensable to a critic — English newspapers — The *Telegraph* and the *Times* — His American experiences — His personal charm — Tributes of Mr. John Morley, Augustine Birrell, and William Watson — Poems — Arnold's place as a poet — Examples of his poems — General estimate of his own and his father's services to English education — Rugby Chapel 241

INTRODUCTORY NOTE.

IN the Catalogue of the British Museum Library, there are no less than eighty-nine entries under the name of Matthew Arnold, and sixty-seven under that of his father. These entries include references to each of the several editions of their published works, whether books or pamphlets, and also to numerous tracts and essays containing criticism or comment upon those works. They do not, however, include the large number of reviews and articles which occur in the periodicals and dictionaries of the time, and which throw light on the character and achievements of the Arnolds. Of the abundant literature with which their names have thus come to be associated, much is occupied with ephemeral controversy, and with incidents little likely to interest the coming generation of readers or indeed to be wholly intelligible to them. It has seemed to me, therefore, that as both men have exerted a large share of influence in forming the opinion of the country on educational questions, and as their lives possess peculiar interest for those who are teachers by profession, there was room for a small volume which, without professing to furnish a new biography, or a new theory respecting either writer, should essay the modest task of bringing together so much of the teaching of both as was likely to prove of permanent value, and also to explain and justify the honourable position the Arnolds occupy in the history of public education in England and in the grateful memory of her teachers. I can claim no higher qualification for this duty than is implied in the facts that I have learned some of the best lessons of my life from the study of these authors; that as a colleague in the Education Department I had many opportunities of knowing Matthew Arnold's views and estimating his personal influence; and that, although for different reasons, I have a genuine admiration for both father and son.

September, 1897.

THOMAS AND MATTHEW ARNOLD

CHAPTER I

Difficulties of biography — How Stanley's *Life of Arnold* has surmounted them — Chief incidents of Arnold's life — Influences which shaped his character — Ships and warfare — Literary revival — History and politics — School-boy experience — Religious doubts and difficulties — Evidential theology — His intellectual outfit generally

THOMAS ARNOLD has had the good fortune to be the subject of one of the best biographies in our language. In the history of English literature, when one comes to enumerate the most notable biographies which have been produced, it will be found that the number of such books entitled to the highest rank as works of art is not large. It is easy to record the dates and parentage, the public employments, the events and movements of a man's outward life, to give a selection from his letters and to add a critical account of his principal writings. But it is not easy to present a true portraiture of the hero's character, to acquire a keen insight into the motive forces of his life, to distinguish the significant from the insignificant, the typical from the exceptional incidents in his career, to look at him from without, and also to understand him from within, and to know with what eyes he saw the world around him, and in what spirit he encountered the problems it presented. "I have remarked," says Carlyle, "that a true delineation of the smallest man, and his scene of pilgrimage through life, is capable of interesting the greatest man; and that all men are to an unspeakable degree brothers, each man's life a strange emblem of every man's, and that human portraits faithfully drawn are of all pictures the welcomest on human walls."[1] Of English books which have best fulfilled these conditions Bacon's *Henry VII.*, Walton's *Lives*, Johnson's *Lives*, Boswell's *Johnson*, Carlyle's *Life of Sterling*, Trevelyan's *Life of Macaulay*, Mr. John Morley's *Rousseau* and *Walpole* are among the best. But Dean Stanley's *Life and Correspondence of Dr. Arnold* will ever be entitled to a high rank, not only for the vividness of its presentation of a striking character and the circumstances of a life, but also for the skill with which relevant and irrelevant facts are discriminated, and for the profound sympathy of the author with its subject. The book will long remain to the student of the social, religious, and political history of the former half of the nineteenth century a treasury of valuable material, because it portrays in clear outline a central figure round which clustered some of the most remarkable personages and incidents of a stirring and eventful period. Stanley's book is a large one and deals necessarily with much ephemeral controversy, religious and political, which

---

[1] Carlyle's *Life of Sterling*, Chap. I.

may possibly not excite any strong interest in the present generation of readers. It is to be feared that these facts may have the effect of concealing from those readers much that is of permanent value in Arnold's history and performance. A smaller volume, *The Life of Dr. Arnold*, by Miss Emma J. Worboise, is also distinguished by care and sympathy, by a reverent and yet candid estimate of character, and especially by the emphasis with which she dwells on the religious side of Arnold's nature and influence. It is not in the vain hope of adding new material to the story which has twice been so well told, or with a view to present any new theory by which to interpret the significance of Arnold's career, that the present book is written, but simply in order to bring into special prominence those features of his own character and that of his more gifted son Matthew, which possess special interest and are likely to be of permanent value to the professional teacher.

Of his personal history during the forty-seven years in which he lived, a brief outline will here suffice. He was born in 1795, at West Cowes in the Isle of Wight, the son of a collector of customs, who died suddenly when the boy was five years old, from the same malady — *angina pectoris* — which afterwards proved fatal to himself. He owed much of his early education to the pious care of his mother, and more to the wisdom and unfailing devotion of his aunt, Miss Delafield, towards whom he through life evinced the strongest affection and gratitude. From 1803 to

1807 he was a pupil in the endowed school at Warminster, and was then transferred to Winchester. In 1811, at the age of sixteen, he was entered at Oxford as a scholar of Corpus Christi College. Three years later he took his degree, and gained a First Class in Classics. In 1815 he was elected a Fellow of Oriel; in 1815 he won the Chancellor's prize for Latin, and in 1817 that for an English essay. He continued in the University until 1820 at work as a tutor, having been ordained two years earlier. He then left Oxford and took a curacy at Laleham in Surrey, married Mary Penrose, and during the next eight years was chiefly occupied in historical studies and in preparing private pupils for the University. In 1828 he accepted the Head-Mastership of Rugby School, and continued in that post until his sudden death in 1842.

Of the influences which contributed to shape his character in early life, perhaps the most potent, next to those of a happy, intelligent, well-ordered home, were the political and military events which at a crisis of extraordinary interest in English history, were well calculated to fire the imagination and call forth the latent patriotism of a young boy. He was but a little child when Pitt was at the zenith of his power, and

> "Launched that thunderbolt of war
> On Egypt, Hafnia, Trafalgar,"

when Nelson's victories filled all English hearts with exultation, when the name of Buonaparte was so associated with terror and alarm that nurses used to frighten children with the threat that he was coming; and when every gazette brought exciting news of battle by field or at sea. The news of Trafalgar to a boy of ten, and of Corunna four years later, and the succession of peninsular victories ending at Vittoria in 1813, could not fail to make an enduring impression on the mind of an open-hearted, thoughtful lad, habitually predisposed to look upon human history rather as the scene of action and of noble endeavour than in any other light.

Years after, he looked back and counted his early experience of ships and warfare as among the formative influences of his life. "More than half my boys," he said in 1829, "never saw the sea and never were in London, and it is surprising how the first of these disadvantages interferes with their understanding much of the ancient poetry. Brought up myself in the Isle of Wight, amidst the bustle of soldiers and sailors, and familiar from a child with boats and ships and the flags of half Europe, which gave me an instinctive acquaintance with geography, I quite marvel to find in what a state of ignorance boys are at seventeen or eighteen who have lived all their days in inland parishes or small country towns."[1]

To such experience, and to the events of the great war, may be attributed the zest with which he afterwards described the wars of Greece and of Rome, the keen interest with which he traced with Livy the march of Hannibal over the Alps, or described the

[1] Letter XII.

battle of Ægospotamos or Salamis. Down to the time when he went to Oxford, all English politics were warlike. Great questions of domestic politics, such as the emancipation of the Catholics, and social and electoral reform, were for the time in abeyance, or they would probably have had, even at that early date, profound interest for him. If the combative instinct was strongly manifest in him through life, so that it is hardly too much to say that in one sense he was a "man of war from his youth," the fact may be partly ascribed to the fierce national rivalries and contests in the midst of which his childhood was passed, and to the strong impulse which those contests gave to his youthful patriotism.

Nor could the changed aspect of the literary horizon be without its influence on a young boy who was from the first a voracious reader, as sensitive to the intellectual as to the political movements of his time. The taste for the classical poetry of Pope and Dryden had declined; Cowper, Thomson, and Crabbe had sought the subjects of their verse in the incidents of familiar life, had evinced a keener sense of the beauties of outward nature, had revolted against established tradition, and had prepared the way for a revival of the healthy romanticism, which was beginning to find a fuller expression in Coleridge, Scott, Wordsworth, and Southey, and was afterwards to achieve some of its greatest triumphs in Tennyson and Browning. But although ballad poetry and Pope's Homer had ever a certain fascination for him, chiefly because of the incidental light it threw on his-

tory, it was not from the poets, ancient or modern, that
he derived the main inspiration of his life. History
and political philosophy always had stronger attrac-
tions for him. Gibbon and Burke, Mitford, Russell,
and Priestley, Thucydides and Livy, Herodotus and
Xenophon, were eagerly read by him at a very early
age, and had a larger share than tragedians or poets
in the direction of his aims and the formation of his
tastes and character. "Every man," says Coleridge,
"is born an Aristotelian or a Platonist. The one
considers reason a quality or attribute, the other considers it a power." We may well hesitate to accept
Coleridge's rough classification of mankind as ex-
haustive; but in so far as the distinction on which
he insists is real, it is well illustrated in Arnold's
mind and character. He was Aristotelian, mainly in
the sense in which he sought to make all speculative
enquiry subservient to the solution of practical problems. To the last he had a peculiar reverence and
affection for the "dear old Stagyrite," and when the
time came for him to send his sons to the University,
he was led to prefer Oxford, because there Aristotle
was held in higher esteem and was more likely to
be well studied than at the sister University. The
parent of science, properly so called, the master of
criticism, and in one sense the founder of formal
logic, Aristotle was to Arnold something more than
all this; he was the guide to right methods of study,
the seer who beheld the larger problems of life, of
society, and of polity in their true perspective, and the
intrepid and earnest seeker after truth. Mr. Justice

Coleridge, in his interesting reminiscences of Arnold as an undergraduate at Corpus, remarks, "He was so imbued with Aristotle's language and ideas that in earnest and unreserved conversation or in writing, his train of thoughts was so affected by the *Ethics* and the *Rhetoric*, that he cited the maxims of the Stagyrite as oracles, and his language was quaintly and easily pointed with phrases from him. I never knew a man who made such familiar, even fond, use of an author; it is scarcely too much to say that he spoke of him as of one intimately and affectionately known and valued."[1]

For one who was destined many years later to exert so large an influence on the public[2] schools of England, it was a happy and appropriate circumstance that his own early education was obtained at public schools and largely influenced by the traditions of venerable endowments. From the age of eight to nearly twelve, he was at Warminster, one of the minor grammar schools, founded early in the eighteenth century; and thenceforward, until the age of sixteen, he was a scholar at Winchester. There is

---

[1] Stanley's *Life and Correspondence*.
[2] This title, "Public Schools," is one which may easily be misinterpreted by American readers, since in their country it connotes the ordinary common and municipal school, which is accessible to all classes, and in which instruction of the most elementary character is given. But in England the common use of the name is limited to ten or fifteen schools of the highest rank and the closest relation to the Universities, and for the most part of ancient and historic foundation, — Eton, Harrow, Winchester, Westminster, St. Paul's, Charterhouse, Merchant Taylor's, Rugby, and Shrewsbury being the most famous examples of the "Public School" type.

little to be recorded respecting his residence at the former of these schools, except that he always spoke gratefully of the obligations he owed to Dr. Griffiths, the head master. But his residence at Winchester had a far larger share in determining the future development of his tastes and the aims of his life. The oldest, nearly the richest, and in many respects the most illustrious, of the public schools of England, Winchester is specially fortunate, not only in its situation and its surroundings, but in its history and traditions. The memory of William of Wykeham, scholar, architect, bishop, and benefactor, the association of the College with the noble Cathedral, the nave of which he had designed, and with New College, Oxford, also a monument of his genius and his munificence, the long roll of famous pupils, which in the course of more than four centuries has contained the names of Chichele, of Warham, Waynflete, of Ken, and of South among ecclesiastics; of Cole, Grocyn, and Udal among scholars; and of Sir Thomas Browne, Sir Henry Wotton, Otway, Young, Collins, and Warton among other notable men in literature or in public life,—all combined to strengthen in him that feeling of reverence for what is ancient and noble, and that pride in a great intellectual inheritance, which form such potent factors in the education of a youth, especially of one filled with ardour and sensibility, and with a desire to do something worthy of his spiritual ancestry. In the massive architecture of the Cathedral, in its solemn mediæval surroundings, in the neighbouring hospital of

Saint Cross, and in the buildings of the ancient College itself, there was much to kindle the imagination of one who loved history; and in the fair and pleasant country round, watered by the Itchen, and beautified by shady elms, there was room for delightful rambles, scope for boyish enterprise, and much to encourage that love of nature which afterwards showed itself to be one of his healthiest characteristics, and which exercised a purifying influence on the whole of his life. To the last he was a loyal Wykehamist, proud of his association with Winchester, grateful to the memory of Goddard and Gabell, who had been head masters during his stay, and steadfastly attached to the friends whom he had made while at school.

No estimate of the intellectual and moral equipment with which he embarked on the voyage of active life would be complete if it did not take into account the deep seriousness of his character, his strong interest in religious questions, and his high sense of duty and of human responsibility. Sir John Coleridge's letter, already quoted, contains a striking record of the impression he made on that acute observer and sympathetic friend, when he was an undergraduate at Corpus, and afterwards Fellow of Oriel.

"His was an anxiously inquisitive mind, a scrupulously conscientious heart: his enquiries previously to his taking orders led him on to distressing doubts on certain points in the Articles; these were not low nor rationalistic in their tendency according to the bad sense of that term, there was no indisposition in him to believe merely because the Article transcended his reason : he doubted the proof and the interpretation of the textual authority. His state was very painful, and I think morbid, for I remarked that the two occasions on which I was privy to the distress were precisely those in which to doubt was against his dearest schemes of worldly happiness; and the consciousness of this seemed to make him distrustful of the arguments which were intended to lead his mind to acquiescence."

A friend to whose counsel he had recourse at this crisis, and who had advised him to pause in his enquiries, to seek earnestly for further help and light from above, and meanwhile to turn himself more strongly than ever to the practical duties of life, wrote of him in 1819:

"It is a defect of A.'s mind that he cannot get rid of a certain feeling of objections, and particularly when, as he fancies the bias is so strong upon him to decide one way from interest : he scruples doing what I advise him, which is to put down the objections by main force whenever they arise in his mind ; fearful that in so doing, he shall be violating his conscience for a maintenance sake."

It may well be doubted whether the latter part of this friendly prescription was the best calculated to heal the hurt of a sensitive conscience. But the advice to busy himself in practical work proved very helpful. Little by little, though after severe trials,

> "He fought his doubts and gathered strength,
>   He would not make his judgment blind ;
>   He faced the spectres of the mind —
> And laid them : thus he came at length

"To find a stronger faith his own,
  And power was with him in the night
  Which makes the darkness and the light
  And dwells not in the light alone."[1]

Though doubt was characteristic of him, and was from the nature of his mental constitution inevitable, he could not, like Montaigne, "se reposer tranquillement sur l'oreiller du doute." His mind was averse from suspense, and after much effort he laid hold firmly on the central truths of the Christian revelation, a hold never abandoned or relaxed. Perhaps in arriving at this result he was helped most by Hooker and Butler, whom to the last he held in higher estimation than any other of the English divines, even than Jeremy Taylor, whose genius, no less than his devout aspirations after holiness, he greatly admired. He certainly owed little to Paley's evidences, or any of the colder evidential theology of the eighteenth century. Very sadly, he said in late life in reference to his youthful studies:[2] "There appears to me in the English divines a want of believing or of disbelieving anything, because it is true or false. It is a question which does not seem to occur to them." This sentence is characteristic of the impatience with which he always treated what seemed to him insincere or half-hearted attempts to defend the Christian faith. His passionate desire to see clearly into the truth of things, and to brush away all hindrances and prejudices by which counsel might

---

[1] *In Memoriam.* [2] Stanley, Letter CLII.

be darkened, alarmed the more timid and orthodox of his companions, but nevertheless led some of them to admit that one had better have Arnold's doubts than most men's certainties.

Thus the environment of his early years and the mental and spiritual outfit with which he entered upon the duties of his life were in many ways happily adapted to the part he was destined to play in the world. Without fortune, but with all the comforts and shelter of a godly home, he was free from any temptation to idleness or extravagance, and conscious from the first that his future was to be assured only by his own strenuous effort. Without patronage or the help of influential friends, he was enabled to breathe the atmosphere of a renowned public school, and to make valuable friendships there. With tastes especially directed towards history and language, and to ethical and political problems, his studies were precisely such as had the closest relation to a profession in which the formation of character is of no less importance than the communication of knowledge. And the fact that his religious convictions had been reached after dear`·
bought spiritual experience, helped all through to place him in sympathy with young and ea·
enquirers, to make him understand their diffic
and to qualify him for the office of a teacher
guide. To be fortunate in the circumstances
the discipline of early life is the lot of ma
But it is the lot of comparatively few to fin(
days such singular opportunities as Arnol(

of turning this discipline to useful account, or to be so strongly and so early penetrated with a sense of the obligation which the possession of privileges entails.

CHAPTER II

Residence at Oxford — Arnold's friends and associates — Marriage and settlement at Laleham — Life as a private tutor — Studies and literary work — Aims and aspirations — Appointment to Rugby

THE period of Arnold's residence at Oxford — 1811-1820 — was one of great intellectual activity and even of unrest. It was indeed anterior to the time of Royal Commissions and of schemes for academic reorganization, for the revival of the professoriate, or for the introduction of new systems of graduation and examination. The importunate claims of the physical sciences for fuller recognition, either in the teaching or the examinations of the Universities, had not yet been urged, and had they been put forth at the time would have met with scant sympathy, either from the most influential leaders of thought in academic circles, or from Arnold himself. He had been elected scholar at Corpus Christi College on his admission to the University; but after taking his degree in the first class in 1814, he became a Fellow of Oriel, and it was in this college that his chief academic friendships were formed. Dean Boyle, in his *Reminiscences*, says, "Many years ago Matthew Arnold said to me that he had been very much struck, in reading again Stanley's life of his father, with the high-minded religious tone of the Corpus set, as they were called, and the great interest shown by them in literature."[1] Whateley, Copleston, Davison, Keble, Hawkins, and Hampden were among the Fellows of Oriel. Arnold obtained the Chancellor's prize for two University essays, Latin and English, but failed to obtain the prize for verse. What are now called educational problems did not possess very great interest in such a society. The principles of political and theological science, and their application to the social problems and the moral needs of the people, were, it would seem, the dominant subjects of thought and discussion in the common room at Oriel. Many of the residents were, as Sir John Coleridge said:

"For the most part Tories in Church and State, great respecters of things as they were, and not very tolerant of the disposition which Arnold brought with him to question their wisdom. Many and long were the conflicts we had and with unequal numbers. There can be little doubt that his rather pugnacious Radicalism and his hatred of the corrupt French Aristocracy often betrayed him into intemperate speech, and placed him out of sympathy with many of his associates, but as he afterwards said, 'All the associations of Oxford, which I loved exceedingly, blew my Jacobinism to pieces.'"

And in a letter to Mr. Tucker[2] he afterwards said:

"The benefits which I have received from my Oxford friendships have been so invaluable, as relating to points of the highest importance, that it is impossible for me ever to forget them, or to cease to look on them as the greatest blessings I have ever yet enjoyed in life."

[1] Reminiscences of Dean Boyle, p. 129. [2] Stanley, Letter IV.

Yet it would not be right to credit Winchester and Oxford with the whole of his education. The strivings and controversies of the school and the University were very precious parts of the discipline which helped to form his opinions and to give courage and force to his mode of expressing them. But experiences of another kind were needed to mature his character and to shape the course of his life, —

"Impulses of deeper birth
Had come to him in solitude," —

or rather in the comparative solitude of Laleham, to which he betook himself in 1819. He had been ordained the year before, and he accepted a curacy in this little village, intending to take as pupils a small number of young men preparing for the Universities. During the seven years succeeding his marriage in 1820 he lived in retirement, busy first with his pupils, and afterwards with a Lexicon to Thucydides and with Greek and Roman history. A pupil who read with him at Laleham, and resided in his house, Mr. Bonamy Price, subsequently a Rugby master, and afterwards Professor of Political Economy at Oxford, testifies: "The most remarkable thing, which struck me at once on joining the Laleham circle, was the wonderful healthiness of tone and feeling which prevailed in it. . . . Arnold's great power as a private tutor resided in this, that he gave such an intense earnestness to life. Every pupil was made to feel that there was a work for him to do, that his happiness as well as his duty lay in doing that work well."

On the very attractive picture which is presented in Dean Stanley's pages of the tranquil life during nearly nine years at Laleham, of his happy domestic surroundings, and of his diligent reading, it is unnecessary here to dwell. It will suffice to say that the interval of comparative seclusion between the active and quasi-public life of the University, and the yet more formidable storm and stress which awaited him at Rugby, did much to strengthen his character, to give solidity to his scholarship, and to deepen his religious convictions. The charm of the country, the delights of home, the daily call of duty, and the refreshment of congenial studies gave fulness and variety to his life, and made up a peaceful and appropriate scene for "those quiet efforts of self-mastery — moral and intellectual — which so well precede in men of a certain strength the going forth to the real business of life and to the contact of good and evil."[1] He himself afterwards spoke of Laleham as a "place of premature rest." The arrangement which he made for the division of duty between himself and his partner practically confined his own attention to the elder pupils; and in making it, he showed a characteristic unwillingness to undertake any duty which he did not feel able to do well. For example:

"Buckland is naturally fonder of the school and is inclined to give it the greatest part of his attention; and I from my Oxford habits as naturally like the other part of

[1] See *Edinburgh Review*, October, 1844.

the business best; and thus I have extended my time of reading with our four pupils before breakfast, from one hour to two. Not that I dislike being in the school, but quite the contrary: still, however, I have not the experience in that sort of work, nor the perfect familiarity with my grammar requisite to make a good master, and I cannot teach Homer as well as my friends Herodotus and Livy, whom I am now reading I suppose for the fiftieth time."[1]

The distrust of his own power to interest boys led him to decline a friendly proposal that he should accept an assistant-mastership at Winchester. "It is a situation," he said, "which I know myself very ill-qualified to fill. . . . I know pretty well what the life of a master at Winchester would be, and feel equally certain that it would be, for me, excessively disagreeable."[2] This, however, was written in 1819, at the beginning of his residence at Laleham. How the experience of the following years helped to alter his estimate of his own powers and duties, and to give him the confidence needed for the main work of his life, may be judged from a few brief sentences extracted from letters written within that period:

"I am now working at German in good earnest, and have got a master who comes down here to me once a week. I have read a good deal of Julius Hare's friend Niebuhr, and have found it abundantly overpay the labour of learning a new language, — to say nothing of some other very valuable books with which I am becoming acquainted, all preparatory to my Roman History. I am going to set to work at the *Coke upon Littleton* of Roman Law to make myself

[1] Letter to J. T. Coleridge, Nov. 29, 1819.
[2] Letter to F. C. Blackstone, Oct. 28, 1819.

acquainted, if possible, with the tenure of property; and I think I shall apply to you for the loan of some of your books touching the Civil law, and especially Justinian's *Institutes*. As my knowledge increases, I only get a clearer insight into my ignorance, and this excites me to do my best to remove it before I descend to the Avernus of the press. But I am twice the man for labour that I have been lately, for the last year or two, because the pupils, I thank God, are going on well. I have at this moment the pleasure of seeing three of them sitting at the round table in the drawing-room, all busily engaged about their themes. The general good effect of their sitting with us all the evening is really very surprising." [1]

"What I am doing in Greek and Roman history" (he is referring to the articles he was preparing for the *Encyclopædia Metropolitana*) "is only my amusement during the single hour of the day that I can employ on any occupation of my own, namely between nine and ten in the evening. With such limited time it would be ridiculous to attempt any work which required much labour and which could not be promoted by my common occupations with my pupils. The Grecian history is just one of the things I can do most easily. My knowledge of it beforehand is pretty full, and my lectures are continually keeping the subject before my mind, so that to write about it is really my recreation; and the Roman history is the same to me, though in a less degree. I could not have any other subject which is equally familiar, or which in my present circumstances would be practicable; and certainly if I can complete plain and popular histories of Greece and Rome of a moderate size, cleared of nonsense and non-Christian principles, I do not think I shall be amusing myself ill." [2]

[1] Letter to W. Hull, Sept. 30, 1824.
[2] Letter to J. Tucker, Oct. 21, 1822.

"It has been my wish to avoid giving my pupils any Greek to do on Sunday, so that we do Greek Testament on other days, but on the Sunday always do some English book, and they read so much; then I ask them questions on it. But I find it almost impossible to make them read a mere English book with sufficient attention to enable them to answer questions out of it, or if they do cram themselves for the time, they are sure to forget it directly after."

"I cannot tell you how the present state of the country occupies my mind, and what a restless desire I feel that it were in my power to do any good."[1]

"I hope to be allowed before I die to accomplish something on Education, also with regard to the Church — the last indeed, even more than the other, were not the last, humanly speaking, so hopeless."[2]

"What say you to a work on πολιτική in the old Greek sense of the word, in which I should try to apply the principles of the Gospel to the legislation and administration of a state?"[3]

"How pure and beautiful was John Keble's article on Sacred Poetry for the *Quarterly*, and how glad I am that he was prevailed upon to write it. It seemed to me to sanctify in a manner the whole number. Mine on the early Roman history was slightly altered by Coleridge here and there, so that I am not quite responsible for all of it."[4]

Ideals and aspirations thus formed and cherished would not long have been satisfied with the restricted area of activity which Laleham afforded; and when, in 1827, Dr. Wooll resigned the Head-Mastership of

---

[1] Letter to G. Cornish, Dec. 6, 1820.
[2] Stanley, pp. 37, 38, 39.
[3] Letter to Whateley, 1827.
[4] Letter to J. Tucker, Aug. 22, 1825.

Rugby, the prospect of succeeding to that office was not only opportune but peculiarly welcome. Among the testimonies in his favour, probably the weightiest was that of his old associate at Oriel, Dr. Hawkins, the Provost, who gave it as his opinion, that "if Arnold were elected, he would change the face of education all through the public schools of England." He himself was not without misgivings about his own adequacy for the task, but was nevertheless conscious of powers which had not yet found their fullest exercise, and he responded with characteristic courage and eagerness to what seemed to him the call of duty. Before the election, he wrote, "If I do get it, I feel as if I could set to work very heartily, and, with God's blessing, I should like to try whether my notions of Christian education are really impracticable, whether our system of public schools has not in it some noble elements, which, under the blessing of the Spirit of all holiness and wisdom, might produce fruit even to life eternal. When I think about it thus, I really long to take rod in hand; but when I think of the πρὸς τὸ τέλος, the perfect vileness which I must daily contemplate, the certainty that this can only be partially remedied, the irksomeness of '*fortemque Gyan, fortemque Cloanthum*,' and the greater form and publicity of the life we should there lead . . . I grieve to think of the possibility of a change."[1]

He was elected to the Head-Mastership of Rugby on Dec. 2, 1827.

---

[1] **Letter to G. Cornish, Nov. 30, 1827.**

After the election his letters have a more reassuring tone. "I have long since looked upon Education as my business in life. . . . You know that I never ran down public schools in the lump, but grieved that their exceeding capabilities were not turned to better account, and if I find myself in time unable to mend what I consider faulty in them, it will at any rate be a practical lesson to teach me to judge charitably of others who do not reform public institutions as much as is desirable."[1] And in writing to J. T. Coleridge, he says: "John Keble is right, it is good for us to leave Laleham, because I feel that we were daily getting to regard it as too much of a home. I cannot tell you how much we both love it, and its perfect peace seems at times an appalling contrast to the publicity of Rugby. I am sure that nothing could stifle this regret, were it not for my full consciousness that I have nothing to do with rest here, but with labour; and then I can and do look forward to the labour with nothing but satisfaction, if my health and faculties be still spared to me."

The trustees of the school, who were chiefly noblemen and country gentlemen of Warwickshire, of whom no one was personally known to Arnold, elected him to the office when he was thirty-one years of age, and he entered on his new duties in the August of 1828. The school had then the reputation of being the lowest and most Bœotian of English public schools; perhaps it was for

[1] Letter to F. C. Blackstone, March 14, 1828.

that very reason that it offered a larger field for the ambition of a new man filled with ideas and theories of his own, and conscious of his power to realize them.

CHAPTER III

Rugby and its foundation—Characteristics of ancient endowed grammar school—Illustrations from statutes of Archbishop Grindal and Dean Colet—The theory of classical education—Milton and the Humanists—Example of an entrance examination—Arnold's scheme of instruction—Latin and Greek not useless, even though forgotten in later life—Evils of mechanical routine—Composition exercises—Versification—Objections to it—School-boy artifices for evading it—Construing—Bowyer of Christ's Hospital—Translation—Grammar and philosophy means not ends—Socratic questioning—General characteristics of Arnold's methods

LAWRENCE SHERIFF, grocer, in 1567 left land and some property in Middlesex to maintain a "fair and convenient schoolhouse at Rugby." Half a century before, Erasmus had been lecturing on Greek at Cambridge, and had advised his friend, Colet, in respect to the foundation of St. Paul's School in London. Within that interval no fewer than one hundred and thirty-seven endowed grammar schools had been founded, including Manchester, Bosworth, Durham, Chester, Warwick, Ipswich, Skipton, Norwich, Sherborne, Louth, Sedbergh, Birmingham, Leeds, Shrewsbury, Christ's Hospital, Tonbridge, Ripon, York, Westminster, Bristol, Merchant Taylor's, Highgate, Bedford, and Richmond. Some of these had been founded by Henry VIII., Edward VI., or Elizabeth, and endowed with the property of dissolved monasteries. Others owed their origin to ecclesiastical corporations, but for the most part they were the product of private munificence, whether of scholars, like Dean Colet and Archbishop Holgate, or traders, like Sir Andrew Judd of Tonbridge and Lawrence Sheriff of Rugby. These men had been profoundly influenced by the new hopes and prospects of learning which characterized the period of the Renaissance and the Reformation, and desired to make permanent provision for instruction in the Greek and Latin tongues, then the only learning which had been formulated and reduced to a system. The record of the development and increasing wealth and repute of Sheriff's foundation will be found at length in Carlisle's *Endowed Grammar Schools*,[1] 1818, and in Mr. Thomas Hughes' lucid and interesting sketch in *Great Public Schools*. The most important material additions to the ground and to the building and its equipment were made by the trustees during the mastership of Dr. John Wooll, Arnold's immediate predecessor, who presided over the school from 1810 till 1827. Of him Mr. Hughes says: "My own belief is that Wooll was a kindly gentleman and a good scholar and teacher, but a choleric as well as exceed-

[1] It is again necessary to guard against the misleading associations which, with American readers, may possibly be connected with this name. In the United States the grammar school is simply the upper department of an ordinary public elementary school, and is distinctly inferior to a "high" or secondary school. But in England the name is generally understood to apply to those institutions, generally some centuries old, which were founded expressly for instruction in the Latin and Greek languages, and were designed to prepare scholars for the Universities.

ingly vigorous little Hercules in black tights, who brought from Winchester the faith that the *argumentum baculinum* is a necessary supplement to 'manners' in the 'making of men' who are to construe Greek plays and write Latin longs and shorts. As to the rest, the discipline of the school and boarding-houses, and any kind of supervision over the boys' life and habits, there were really none, except that missing a 'calling over' entailed a certain flogging. They were left to themselves, with the inevitable result. As specimens of the condition of things which his successor had to deal with, I may mention that beagles and guns were kept by the sportsmen among the big fellows, and that those whose tastes turned that way had private cellars in the studies."[1]

The worthy Lawrence Sheriff, it must be remembered to his honour, did not attempt to impose upon his successors any educational theories of his own, or any restrictions as to the aims or methods which should be pursued in the school. The trustees were enjoined in the paper annexed to his will to procure an "honest, discrete, and learned man, being a Master of Arts to take charge of the house as a Free Grammar School," and this was a sufficient description well understood in his day of the kind of institution he desired to endow. Other "pious founders," with less modesty, and a more limited view of the possibilities of the future, had prescribed with curious minuteness, not merely the subjects and the order of studies, but even the books which should be used and

[1] *Great Public Schools*, p. 148.

the hours at which lessons should be begun and ended as well as the scholarly and other qualifications which the head master and his assistants should possess. Two examples of this kind will suffice.

Archbishop Grindal (1583), in the elaborate statutes which he laid down for the free grammar school of St. Bees, prescribed that the schoolmaster should be "a meet and learned person, that can make Greek and Latin verses, and read and interpret the Greek Grammar and other Greek authors." His scheme of instruction, set forth with great minuteness, may be fairly accepted as typical of that conception of a liberal education which prevailed at the end of the sixteenth and beginning of the seventeenth century.

"The schoolmaster shall carefully seek to bring up all his scholars equally in learning and good manners, and shall refuse none being born in the counties of Cumberland and Westmoreland, of whom he shall receive only four pence apiece at their first coming, for the entering of their names into his book, and no more for their teaching. He shall encourage the good natured, and those that are toward in learning, by praising and preferring them to higher places, and shall dispraise and displace the slothful and untoward that either for love of commendation or fear of shame, they may be provoked to learn and profit at their books. He shall chiefly labour to make his scholars perfect in the Latin and Greek grammar, and to the end they may better profit therein, he shall exercise them in the best authors in both tongues that are meet for their capacity. Provided always that the first books of construction that they shall read, either in Latin or Greek, shall be the smaller catechisms set forth by public authority for that purpose in the said tongues, which we will that they shall learn by heart, that with the knowledge of the tongues, they may also learn their duty towards God and man."

Dean Colet (1509) had prescribed for his famous school at St. Paul's, ordinances which furnished a model for many of the sixteenth century foundation deeds and was fairly characteristic of the revived taste for learning which prevailed at that time.

"I will that the children learne first above all the *Catechizon* in Englishe, and after the *Accidens*, that I made or some other, if any be better for the purpose, to induce children more speedily to Latin speche. And then *Institutum Christiani Hominis* which that learned Erasmus made at my request, and the book called *Copia* of the same Erasmus. And then other authors, Christian, as *Prudentius* and *Proba* and *Sedulius* and *Juvencus* and *Baptista Mantuanus*, and such others as shall be thought convenient, and most to purpose unto the true Latin speche. All *Barbary*, all corruption, all Latin adulterate which ignorant blind fooles brought into this world, and with the same hath distayned and poisoned the very Roman tongue which in the time of *Tully* and *Sallust* and *Virgil* and *Terence* was used, which also *St. Jerome* and St. Ambrose and St. Austin and many holy doctors learned in their times, I utterly bannyshe and exclude out of the schole; and charge the Masters that they teche always that is beste and instruct the children in Greke and redynge Latin, in redynge unto them such authors that hath with wisdom joyned the pure chaste eloquence."

"That they teche always that is beste," — This is a high and generous utterance and represents fairly the spirit of the Renaissance and of the founders of grammar schools. It is because Latin and Greek were the best intellectual aids then known, and the keys to all the knowledge then best worth having, that these languages formed the staple of a gentleman's training. No higher conception of a liberal education could possibly be formed than that each age should furnish its youth with its best. But this object is to be attained by imitating the spirit rather than the letter of founder's statutes, and by such a study of the needs and circumstances of our own age as may enable us to do for our contemporaries what Colet and Grindal sought to do for theirs, and what they would probably have done had they lived now.

It cannot be claimed for Arnold that he was eager to emancipate himself from the traditions thus inherited from the sixteenth century. We cannot concede to him the character of a great reformer or revolutionist in the sense in which Comenius, Rousseau, Locke, or Pestalozzi was entitled to one of those designations. He was not a realist, but essentially a "humanist" of the type of Milton. He accepted the traditions of the long succession of English teachers, from Ascham and Colet down to Busby and Keate, in favour of making the study of language, and particularly the languages of Greece and Rome, the staple of a liberal education. But, like Milton, he rebelled strongly against the wooden, mechanical, and pedantic fashion in which those languages were often taught, as if the attainment of proficiency in them were an end in itself and not the means to some higher end. Milton had protested against the "preposterous exactions by which the empty wits of children were forced to compose themes, verses, and orations, which are the acts of ripest judgement; and were thus mocked and deluded with ragged notions and babblements while they expected worthy and delightful knowledge."[1] He would indeed have the pupil introduced to a great variety of Greek and Roman authors, poets, philosophers, and orators, but mainly that through and by means of these writers, he might obtain access to the best thought and culture which the world could afford, and so become acquainted with history and political science, with logic, with the principles of law and morals, with geometry and natural philosophy, with the story of heroes and statesmen, so as to "stir up learners with high hopes of becoming brave men and worthy patriots dear to God and famous to all ages." In like manner Arnold, while founding his whole educational system on the study of the ancient languages, sought mainly to use those languages as instruments for a large extension of the range of subjects beyond the traditional routine. Greek and Latin were to him the $\pi o\hat{v}$ $\sigma\tau\hat{\omega}$, the firm earth on which he sought to erect a fabric in which history, poetry, philosophy, ethics, love of truth, and aspirations after nobleness and usefulness should find their due place.

Accordingly we are not to expect from him any attempt to dissociate himself from the traditional belief of scholars that, after all, knowledge of language was the truest measure of a boy's ability and

[1] Letter to Master Samuel Hartlib.

promise. In classifying new pupils, he would not have cared to adopt the multifarious method of modern entrance examinations, with their options and alternatives. The form into which a new scholar was to be entered was determined by his acquaintance with grammar and vocabulary, and by little else. When the little Arthur Stanley, at the age of thirteen, went up to Rugby, and had concluded his first awful visit to the Doctor, he wrote to his sister Mary, "Papa and I walked to Dr. Arnold's, and presently Mrs. Arnold came in; she was very nice indeed. At last came the Doctor himself, but I certainly should not have taken him for a doctor. He was very pleasant and did not look old. When Papa asked him whether I could be examined, he said that if I would walk into the next room he would do it himself; so of course I went with him, with a feeling like that when I am going to have a tooth drawn. So he took down a Homer, and I read about half a dozen lines, and the same with Virgil; he then asked me a little about my Latin verses, and set me down without more ado in the great book as placed in the fourth form. I felt such a weight off my mind when that was done."[1]

In Arnold's own account of the school, contributed to the *Journal of Education,* 1834, he describes at length its general aims and methods. He sets forth a graduated scheme of instruction extending from the first to the sixth form. It will suffice here to give in

[1] *Life of Dean Stanley*, Vol. I.

detail the course of the first, the fourth, and the sixth, since the character of the intermediate exercises may be readily inferred from them:

CLASSICAL DIVISION.

	Language.	Scripture.	History.
First Form.	Latin Grammar and Delectus.	Church Catechism and Abridgement of New Testament History.	Markham's England.
Fourth Form.	Æschylus, Prometheus. Virgil, Æn. II. and III. Cicero, de Amicitia.	Acts in the Greek Testament. St. John in the English Bible. Old Testament History.	Part of Xenophon's Hellenics. Florus III. to IV. History of Greece, U.K.S. Markham's France from Philip de Valois. Growth of Italy and Germany.
Sixth Form.	Part of Virgil and Homer. One or more Greek Tragedies. Orations of Demosthenes. Cicero against Verres. Part of Aristotle's Ethics.	One of the Prophets in the Septuagint Version. Parts of the New Testament.	Parts of Thucydides and Arian. Parts of Tacitus. Parts of Russell's Modern Europe.

	MATHEMATICAL DIVISION.	FRENCH DIVISION.
First Form.	Tables. Addition to Division. Simple and Compound Reduction.	Hamel's Exercises up to the Auxiliary Verb.

	MATHEMATICAL DIVISION.	FRENCH DIVISION.
FOURTH FORM.	Decimals. Involution and Evolution. Elementary Algebra. Binomial Theorem. Euclid, Book I.	Hamel's Second Part. Syntax of Pronouns. La Fontaine's Fables.
SIXTH FORM.	Euclid III.-VI. Simple and Quadratic Equations. Trigonometry. Conic Sections.	Parts of Guizot's Histoire de la Revolution de l'Angleterre, and Mignet's Histoire de la Revolution Française.

The article proceeds to defend the principle on which so large a proportion of the time and attention are devoted to the Greek and Roman classics. The writer admits frankly that the "first origin of classical education affords in itself no reasons for continuing it now. When Latin and Greek were almost the only written languages of civilized man, it is manifest that they must have furnished the subjects of all liberal education. The question, therefore, is wholly changed since the growth of a complete literature in other languages; since France and Italy and Germany and England have each produced their philosophers, their poets, and their historians worthy to be placed on the same level with those of Greece and Rome." He shows that, "although there is not the same reason now which existed three or four centuries ago for the study of Greek and Roman literature, there are others no less substantial." These reasons he finds in the familiar facts that the grammatical forms of Greek and Latin are at once perfect and incapable of being understood without long and minute attention; that the study of them involves the general principles of grammar, and that their peculiar excellences illustrate the conditions under which language may become clear and forcible and beautiful. And apart from the linguistic training afforded, he set a peculiar value on the general broadening of the intellectual horizon which attended the study of the literature and history of the ancient world.

"Expel Greek and Latin from your schools," he says, "and you confine the views of the existing generation to themselves and their immediate predecessors, you will cut off so many centuries of the world's experience, and place us in the same state as if the human race had first come into existence in the year 1500. . . . Aristotle and Plato and Thucydides and Cicero and Tacitus are most untruly called ancient writers. They are virtually our own countrymen and contemporaries, but have the advantage which is enjoyed by intelligent travellers, that their observation has been exercised in a field out of the reach of common men, and that having thus seen in a manner with our eyes what we cannot see for ourselves, their conclusions are such as bear upon our own circumstances; while their information has all the charm of novelty, and all the value of a mass of new and pertinent facts, illustrative of the great science of the nature of civilized man."

In reply to the familiar argument that men in after life often throw their Greek and Latin aside, and that this fact shows the uselessness of such early studies, the article goes on to emphasize a view which is too often lost sight of in popular discussion, whether in relation to the higher or the lower departments of educational work. It is not uncommon to find critics who seek to discredit the arithmetic and geography and the grammar of the elementary school by urging that much of the knowledge so acquired is soon forgotten. No doubt it is. So is a great part of all the knowledge received by learners at all ages, and in reference to all subjects. But this does not prove that the acquisition is barren or useless. It may not survive in the exact form in which it has been first imparted. But it has for the time served its purpose; it has helped to put the mind into a better attitude for the acquisition of further knowledge, and it has left behind it such a residuum of thought and experience as will make it easy to revert to the subject and learn it anew, if special occasion for it should arise. In fact, nothing which is honestly learned, and which forms a legitimate part of a scheme of instruction having an organic unity and a clear purpose of its own, can ever be rightly regarded as worthless; and no time spent in acquiring such details is ever wasted, even though they may have disappeared from the memory and left no visible result. Arnold's argument was sound and admits of far wider application than to the particular department of education to which he was especially interested. "It does not follow that when a man lays aside his Latin and Greek books, he forgets also all that he had ever gained from them. This, however, is so far from being the case, that even where the results of a classical education are least tangible and least appreciated, even by the individual himself, still the mind often retains much of the effect of its early studies in the general liberality of its tastes and comparative comprehensiveness of its views and actions."

But all this presupposes that the teaching is intelligent and that the teacher has so far emancipated himself from routine as to be able to discriminate between what is mechanical and sterile, and that which is formative and vital in the classical tradition. The mere scholar, he contended, cannot possibly communicate to his pupils the main advantage of a classical education.

"The knowledge of the past is valuable, because without it our knowledge of the present and of the future must be scanty: but if the knowledge of the past be confined wholly to itself: if instead of being made to bear upon things around us, it be totally isolated from them, and so disguised by vagueness and misapprehension as to appear incapable of illustrating them, then indeed it becomes little better than laborious trifling, and they who declaim against it may be fully forgiven."[1]

The characteristic of Arnold as a schoolmaster was that he was much more concerned to put new life, freshness, and meaning into the received methods than to invent new ones. What is imitable in his system — if system it may be called — is not a new educational creed or practice, but the infusion into the system of a new spirit, one of enthusiasm, of clear insight into the inner intellectual and moral needs of scholars, and of careful introspection in reference to those studies which had enriched his

[1] Arnold's *Miscellaneous Works*, p. 350.

own character and intellect most. Dean Stanley says of him, "He was the first Englishman who drew attention in our public schools to the historical, political, and philosophical value of philology and of the ancient writers as distinguished from the mere verbal criticism and elegant scholarship of the last century." This may be illustrated in his treatment of composition exercises, of which he says:

"There are Exercises in Composition in Greek and Latin prose, Greek and Latin verse, and English prose as in other large classical schools. In the subjects given for original composition in the higher forms there is a considerable variety, — historical descriptions of any remarkable events, geographical descriptions of countries, imaginary speeches and letters supposed to be spoken or written on some great question, or under some memorable circumstances; etymological accounts of words in different languages, and criticisms on different books are found to offer an advantageous variety to the essays on moral subjects to which the boy's prose composition has sometimes been confined."[1]

Dean Stanley gives in an interesting appendix a selection of the themes chosen for composition exercises, from which a few characteristic examples may be cited here:

(*a*) The differences between advantages and merits.

(*b*) Conversation between Thomas Aquinas, James Watt, and Walter Scott.

(*c*) The principal events and men of England, France, and Germany and Holland A.D. 1600.

[1] *Quarterly Journal of Education*, 1834.

(d) How far the dramatic faculty is compatible with a love of truth.

(e) De seculo, quo Esais vaticinia sua edidit.

It will be seen that there is very little of the iconoclastic temper in this description of his methods. He did not even attack the time-honoured superstition that the manufacture of Latin and Greek verses was the ultimate test and crown of scholarship. It is true he did not like it. He rebelled, as Milton did, against a theory which imposed on young boys a task for which they were wholly unfit; he was conscious of the preposterous absurdity of regarding the fitting together of longs and shorts as a true *Gradus ad Parnassum*, but he nevertheless sought to make the best of the method and to clothe the dry bones with flesh and blood.

But it may be doubted whether he ever fully realized the enormous injury done to the rank and file of boys by this antiquated and soulless exercise; the inevitable weariness and disgust produced by it; the false and ignoble ideal of scholarship which it set before them, or the intellectual habits which it generates. An eminent public schoolmaster of a later generation has had the courage to speak with great frankness on this point. He says:

"Without a conception of rhythm, without a gleam of imagination, without a touch of fancy, boys are set down to write verses, and these verses are to be in an unknown tongue in which they scarcely possess a germ of the scantiest vocabulary, or a mastery of the most simple construction; and further, it is to be in strict imitation of poets of whom, at their best, they have only read a few score of lines. . . . The pupil is required under all the inexorable exigencies of metre to reproduce in artificial and phraseological Latin the highly elaborate thoughts of grown men, to piece their mutilated fancies, and reproduce their fragmentary conceits. In most cases the very possibility of doing so depends on his hitting upon a particular epithet, which presents the requisite combination of longs and shorts, or on his evolving some special and often recondite turn of thought and expression. Supposing, for instance (to take a very easy line, typical of many thousands of lines), he has to write a pentameter.

'Where Acheron rolls waters.'

He will feel that his entire task is to write where *something* Acheron rolls *something* waters. His one object is to get in the *something* which shall be of the right shape to screw into the line. The epithet may be ludicrous; it may be grotesque, but provided he can make his brick he does not trouble himself about the quality of his straw, and it matters nothing to him, if it be a brick such as could not by any possibility be used in any human building. It is a literal fact, that a boy very rarely reads through the English he is doing, or knows, when it has been turned into Latin, what it is all about; hence, for the next year or two his life resolves itself into a boundless hunt after epithets of the right shape, to be screwed into the greatest number of places; a practice exactly analogous to the putting together of Chinese puzzles, only producing a much less homogeneous and congruous result."[1]

Whatever may be urged in favour of the theory of verse composition as a youthful effort of imagination, as a discipline in taste and literary discrimination,

---

[1] Dean Farrar in *Essays on a Liberal Education*, p. 213.

or in the right choice and use of words, there can be no doubt that in practice the "sad mechanic exercise" is wearisome and uninspiring, and involves an appalling waste of time. There was, for example, a common form of exercise, called a "vulgus," a subject being given out, and a fixed number of eight or ten lines being required to be produced and recited in class next morning. There was also in common use a collection of traditionary vulguses, consisting of past exercises copied and accumulated and used over and over again with small and colourable alterations. Even those boys who did the work honestly cared for little except to piece together a few lines which would scan tolerably; but many omitted to take the trouble, and got younger and cleverer boys to write for them. Like all forms of teaching which do not awaken the genuine interest of the scholar or challenge his sympathies, the system of compulsory verse-making lends itself with peculiar facility to school-boy artifices and evasive tricks. The copying out of another boy's vulgus or verse exercise, and the surreptitious use of "cribs," became so common that it was very hard even for an honest boy to convince himself that they were wrong. Mr. Hughes, who is certainly not an unfriendly witness where the public school traditions are concerned, puts into the mouth of Harry East, who, on the whole, was meant to represent a lad of average ability, with a code of honour which, if not exalted, was at least respectable, a very brief statement of the school-boy creed on this point:

"It's a fair trial of skill between us and the masters, like a match at football or a battle. We're natural enemies in school, that's a fact. We've got to learn so much Latin and Greek and do so many verses, and they've got to see that we do it. If you can slip the collar and do so much less without getting caught, that's one to us. If they can get more out of you, or catch us shirking, that's one to them. All's fair in war but lying. If I run my luck against theirs and go into school without looking at my lessons, why am I a snob or a sneak? I don't tell the master I have learned it; he's got to find out whether I have or not. What's he paid for? If he calls me up and I get floored, he makes me write it out in Greek and English — very good; he's caught me, and I don't grumble. I grant you, if I go and snivel to him and tell him I've really tried to learn it, but found it so hard without a translation, or say I've had a toothache or any humbug of that kind, I'm a snob — that's my school morality. It's served me for these five years, and it's all clear and fair, no mistake about it. We understand it, and they understand it, and I do not what we are to come to with any other."[1]

It is right, however, to say that later experience modified Arnold's views respecting the educative value of verse-composition. In a letter to Mr. Justice Coleridge in 1833, he said:

"You will be amused when I tell you that I am becoming more and more a convert to the advantages of Latin and Greek verse, and more suspicious of the mere *fact* system; that would cram with knowledge of particular things, and call it information. My own lessons with the Sixth Form are directed now to the best of my power to the furnishing rules or formulæ for them to work with, *e.g.* rules to be

[1] *Tom Brown's School Days*, Chap. VII.

observed in translation, principles of taste as to the choice of English words, as to the keeping or varying idioms and metaphors, etc., or in history, rules of evidence, or general forms for the dissection of campaigns, or the estimating the importance of wars, revolutions, etc. This, together with the opening as it were the sources of knowledge, by telling them where they can find such and such things, and giving them a notion of criticism, not to swallow things whole as the scholars of an earlier period too often did, is what I am labouring at, much more than at giving information. And the composition is mending decidedly, though speaking to an Etonian I am well aware that our amended state would be with you a very degenerate one. But we are looking up certainly, and pains are taking in the Lower Forms, of which we shall, I think, soon see the fruit."[1]

It may well be doubted whether this partial recantation does much to prove that the system was a good one. In teaching, that system which is best administered is best, and Arnold had the power of putting a soul into a method which, in other hands, might prove sterile and mechanical. The arguments against verse-making as an intellectual exercise for common use and under the treatment of average teachers remain unanswered; and their force is nowise diminished by the fact that now and then an enthusiastic and inspiring head master can contrive to make the exercise effective.

To another of the traditional usages of the classical schools — the practice of *construing* — Arnold had less scruple in expressing his emphatic objection. He regarded this form of exercise as another illustration

[1] Letter LXXIV.

of the tendency to neglect the literary art for the sake of those formalities of detail which concern the material form rather than the spiritual meaning of literature. He thought that the efforts of teachers to secure attention to the parts of a sentence often made it difficult for a learner to understand its significance as a whole.

"Every lesson in Greek or Latin," he said, "may, or ought to be made a lesson in English; the translation of every sentence in Demosthenes or Tacitus is properly an exercise in extemporaneous English composition; a problem how to express with equal brevity, clearness, and force in our own language, the thought which the original author has so admirably expressed in his. But the system of construing, far from assisting, is positively injurious to our knowledge and use of English; it accustoms it to a tame and involved arrangement of our words, and to the substitution of foreign idioms in the place of such as are national; it obliges us to caricature every sentence that we render, by turning what is, in its original dress, beautiful and natural, into something which is neither Greek nor English, stiff, obscure, and flat, exemplifying all the faults incident to language and excluding every excellence. The exercise of translation, on the other hand, meaning by translation the expressing of an entire sentence of a foreign language by an entire sentence of our own, as opposed to the rendering separately into English either every separate word, or at most only parts of the sentence, whether larger or smaller, the exercise of translation is capable of furnishing improvement to students of every age according to the measure of their abilities and knowledge."[1]

The whole of the paper from which this extract is

---

[1] The use of the classics — *Miscellaneous Works*, pp. 351 *et seq.*

taken well deserves the attentive study of those
engaged in the teaching of Latin and Greek, as it
illustrates, in several ways, the relation between the
study of separate words and grammatical forms on
the one hand, and the culture of the language faculty
and the development of a true literary taste on the
other. Unless Arnold could establish a real *rapport*
between the learning of an ancient language and a
fuller command of the resources of our own, he was
disposed to regard what is called mere classical learning as a barren and pedantic accomplishment. For
example, he insisted on the importance of following
in English the analogy required by the age and character of the original writer; *e.g.* "In translating
Homer hardly any words should be employed except
Saxon and the oldest and simplest of those which are
of French origin, and the language should consist of
a series of simple propositions connected with one
another only by the most inartificial conjunctions.
In translating the tragedians, the words should be
principally Saxon, but mixed with many of French
or foreign origin, like the language of Shakespeare
and the other dramatists of the reign of Elizabeth
and James I. . . . So, also, in translating the prose
writers of Greece and Rome; Herodotus should be
rendered in the style and language of the chroniclers;
Thucydides in that of Bacon or Hooker; while Demosthenes, Cicero, Cæsar, and Tacitus require a style
completely modern, the perfection of the English language such as we now speak and write it, varied only
to suit the individual differences of the different

writers, but in its range of words, and in its idioms, substantially the same."

It is interesting to compare with these views those of an older schoolmaster, Bowyer, of Christ's Hospital, of whom one of his most illustrious pupils speaks with affectionate gratitude.

"I enjoyed," says Coleridge, "the inestimable advantage of a very sensible, though at the same time a very severe master. He early moulded my taste to the preference of Demosthenes to Cicero, of Homer to Theocritus and Virgil, and again of Virgil to Ovid. He habituated me to compare Lucretius (in such extracts as I then read), Terence, and above all the chaster poetry of Catullus, not only with the Roman poets of the so-called silver and brazen age, but with even those of the Augustan era, and on grounds of plain sense and universal logic to see and assert the superiority of the former in the truth and naturalness both of their thoughts and diction. At the same time that we were studying the Greek tragic poets, he made us read Shakespeare and Milton as lessons, and they were the lessons too which required most time and trouble to bring up so as to escape his censure. I learned from him that poetry, even that of the loftiest and seemingly that of the wildest odes, had a logic of its own as severe as that of science, and more difficult because more subtle, more complex and more dependent on more and more fugitive causes. In the truly great poets he would say, there is a reason assignable not only for every word, but for the position of every word, and I well remember that availing himself of the synonyms to the Homer of Didymus, he made us attempt to show, with regard to each, why it would not have answered the same purpose, and wherein consisted the peculiar fitness of the word in the original text."[1]

[1] Coleridge, *Biographia Literaria*, Chap. I.

It is not to be understood that Arnold's unqualified contempt for the practice of construing, and his preference for translating, represent the final result of all experience in reference to the teaching of a language. The truth is that both processes, in their due measure and proportion, are needed for the thorough comprehension of an ancient author. There can be no real perception of the meaning of a sentence as a whole, unless the learner can, if challenged, explain the significance of each single word and the part it plays in the final result. Readers of Mr. Thring's rather puzzling but inspiring book will remember what importance he attached to what he called "sentence anatomy," and will understand why, in the practice of that famous teacher, the construing lesson assumed greater importance than in Arnold's method. Fundamentally, however, the aims of both teachers were identical. "The ultimate end," said Thring, "of the study of the classics, is to make the learner an artist in words and a conscious master of his own tongue."[1] Arnold regarded the conventional method largely practised in public schools as ill adapted to its professed purpose, and in reply to those who argued that translation without construing led to inaccuracy and slovenliness, urged in the article already quoted, that

"It is a mere chimera to suppose, as many do, that what they call free translation is a convenient cover for inaccurate scholarship. It can only be so through the incompetence or carelessness of the teacher. If the force of every part of

[1] *Theory and Practice of Teaching*, p. 111.

the sentence be not fully given, the translation is so far faulty; but idiomatic translation, much more than literal, is an evidence that the translator does see the force of the original, and it should be remembered that the very object of so translating is to preserve the spirit of an author, when it would be lost or weakened by translating literally; but where a literal translation happens to be faithful to the spirit, then, of course, it should be adopted, and any omission or misrepresentation of any part of the bearing of the original does not preserve its spirit, but, as far as it goes, sacrifices it and is not to be called free translation, but rather imperfect, blundering, or in a word bad translation."

A later writer, distinguished no less by success as a teacher than by an extensive acquaintance with the philosophy of education, has embodied the common-sense view of the whole question in one or two vigorous sentences. Mr. Storr says:

"Let me urge you to set your faces as a rock against the system of literal construing, which not only prevails in most class-rooms, but is even justified and encouraged by pedantic and unscrupulous schoolmasters. The head-masters have lately been telling us that for the classically trained boy English literature is of the nature of a superfluity, a sort of gilding the refined gold of Greek or painting the lily of Latinity, that the best way of learning our native tongue is to learn to translate Thucydides and Cicero, and to turn Shakespeare and Tennyson into Greek iambics and Latin elegiacs. The theory is too ridiculous to need repeating here, and its absurdity is sufficiently demonstrated by the slipshod and ungrammatical English in which some of these classically trained head-masters express their theories on English Composition. And yet it has a foundation of truth, provided always that, for the first stage, idiomatic English is insisted on. No one, after once the sentence had to be analysed, would ever dream of translating literally *Comment vous portez-vous ?* but pedantry will insist on boys rendering year after year Latin historical presents by English presents, Latin ablative absolutes by the absolute construction (that is the commonest of all Latin idioms), by turns which are rare in English and only half naturalised, and representing Greek redundancies by English synonyms."[1]

So, although to the last the study of language appeared to Arnold the best available instrument for the education of mankind, it was not mere grammar or philology which seemed to him the most fruitful part of linguistic discipline, but the indirect effect of the study on the cultivation of studies other than itself. He refused, indeed, to recognize the making of pentameters and sapphics as the highest of human accomplishments, or a false quantity as the unpardonable sin: but by seeking, as he would say, to make his teaching dynamical rather than mechanical, he found in Latin and Greek exercises the means of calling forth power, of cultivating taste and character, right ambition, and interest in great and high themes, to all of which he attached more value than to the learning of a language *per se* or to any mere information. It is very characteristic of him and of his desire to connect the study of the ancient languages with the progress of modern thought, that he expressed a wish for a cheap edition of Bacon's *Instauratio Magna*, and thought he could make it useful not merely in point of Latinity, "by setting fellows to correct the style whenever it was cumbrous

[1] Mr. Francis Storr, in the *Educational Times*, July, 1895.

and incorrect," but also as a means of familiarizing boys with the inductive process and with the temper of mind in which the achievements of modern science could be appreciated.

Like all true teachers, from Socrates downwards, he relied more on questioning than on mere didactics. His whole method, says Dean Stanley, was founded on the principle of awakening the intellect of every individual boy. "As a general rule, he never gave information except as a kind of reward for an answer, and often withheld it altogether or checked himself, in the very act of uttering it, from a sense that those whom he was addressing had not sufficient interest or sympathy to entitle them to receive it. His explanations were as short as possible, enough to dispose of the difficulty and no more; his questions were of a kind to call the attention of the boys to the real point of every subject, and to disclose to them the exact boundaries of what they knew or did not know. With regard to younger boys he said, 'It is a great mistake to think that they should *understand* all they learn; for God has ordered that in youth the memory should act vigorously, independent of the understanding, whereas a man cannot usually recollect a thing unless he understands it.' But in proportion to their advance in the school he tried to cultivate in the boys a habit not only of collecting facts, but of expressing themselves with facility, and of understanding the principles on which the facts rested. 'You come here,' he said, 'not to read, but to learn how to read.' "[1]

[1] Stanley, Chap. III.

On the whole, the student of "methodology" who searches the life of Arnold for tips and artifices whereby classical teaching may be rendered easier or more vital is likely to be disappointed. Whatever was excellent in the Rugby method of classical learning lay rather in the man, and in the spirit in which he worked, than in the communicable form of newly invented original rules and systems. His merit consisted mainly in the fact that he did not mistake means for ends ; that he kept constantly in sight the goal to which all true education should be directed, and that he refused to attach undue importance to conventions and usages which did not help boys to arrive thither. It was, in fact, the cardinal principle, as it was the only justification of all his language exercises, that it was not knowledge, but the appetite for knowledge, and the means of gaining it, which it was the chief business of a schoolmaster to impart.

CHAPTER IV

Language as a discipline contrasted with natural science — Knowledge of physical facts not the only science — History — Relation of Ancient and Modern History — Its claims as a school subject — Training for citizenship — Example of a school exercise — Niebuhr's researches in Roman History — Arnold's own treatment of the regal period of Rome — His love of history infectious — Geography — Thoroughness in teaching — Qualifications of assistants — School organization — Relation of a head master to governing body

IT will thus be seen that Arnold was a faithful representative and successor of the school of educational theorists who place the "humanities" in the foremost place as the staple of liberal culture. He may be said to belong to the pre-scientific era of educational history. Had he lived to know of the marvellous extension of physical science which has characterized the subsequent half-century, had he followed the researches of Huxley and Darwin and Lockyer and Lyell, and recognized the skill with which the forces of nature have been investigated and turned to account in enlarging the resources of human life and happiness, he might in all probability have revised his plans and seen the wisdom of recognizing the claims of natural knowledge as an integral part of a scheme of liberal education. He was too well acquainted with the *Novum Organum*, and with the spirit of its illustrious author, to disregard the new and beautiful knowledge which such studies as biology, chemistry, and zoölogy have of late brought to light. But it may well be doubted whether he would ever have regarded any acquaintance with the material forces of nature as good substitutes for the intellectual culture derived from classical studies, or as equal to them in disciplinal value. It is certain that he would have rebelled against the view put forth by Herbert Spencer in his famous essay, "What knowledge is of most worth?" In particular he would have been unwilling to admit the claims of the physicists to appropriate the name of "science" to their own special department of human learning. Science, in its true sense, connotes organized systematic knowledge, as distinguished from the knowledge of disjointed and unrelated facts. It implies insight into reasons, causes, consequences. It is not specially concerned with one class of phenomena, nor with one subject of investigation, but pertains alike to all branches of knowledge if treated in a philosophic spirit. The nature and significance of the Greek aorist, or the laws of the syllogism, belong as truly to the domain of science as the precession of the equinoxes, or the superposition of strata. It is just as possible to teach grammar and philology in a scientific way as it is to treat biology or the theory of refraction in an unscientific way. Even in an elementary school, the teacher who makes clear the distinction between the subject and the predicate, or between the essential and the non-essential parts of a sentence, is as truly a teacher of science as he who explains why the water boils, or what are the respective functions of the heart and lungs. Our popular conceptions of the relative value of different departments of human knowledge will become clearer when the honoured name of "science" shall have come to be understood to imply rather a sound method of investigating truth than the particular kind of truth which is subject to investigation.

For the present, however, it will suffice to say that "science," in the restricted sense in which we are accustomed to use it of late, hardly came into the Rugby scheme at all. But language, though the centre of that scheme, was not the exclusive subject of instruction. Auxiliary to it, and necessary to give organic unity to the whole plan, were history, geography, divinity, ethical and political science. And of these, history took the foremost place.

The educational value of history, whether ancient or modern, considered as a formative study and a legitimate part of academic discipline, has been much discussed by teachers and theorists. On the one hand, it is contended that the material is unsuited for the purpose of such discipline; that the facts with which it deals are inexact, unverified, and often incapable of verification, and that the sureness and precision which should characterize all scholarship are unattainable in history. And it is often further contended that the subject should not be recognized in the curriculum of a school or a university at all, but should be left for the voluntary reading of the learner. On the other hand, there are those who see in the record of past events, and in the accumulated

experience of mankind, the most awakening form of
intellectual exercise, the best training for citizenship, and some of the profoundest and most potent
truths, in their bearing on human conduct and on the
formation of character. Arnold had no misgivings
as to the side of the controversy on which he should
range himself. Coleridge once complained that the
lessons of history failed to teach us as they might,
because the light which experience gives is little
more to us than a lantern on the stern of a ship,
which illuminates only the waves that are behind us.
It was precisely against this mistake that Arnold's
whole teaching was a practical protest. Freeman's
dictum that "History is past politics, and politics
present history," was well illustrated in the Rugby
lessons. The life of the Commonwealth was to him
the main subject of history; the laws of political science, the main lesson of history; the desire of taking
an active share in the great work of government, the
highest earthly desire of the ripened mind.[1] In the
interesting *Excursus* to be found appended to his
edition of Thucydides, abundant evidence may be
seen of the keen interest Arnold felt in tracing the
analogies between ancient and modern history, and
of his desire to obtain light from the polity and
social life of the Greeks and to cast it upon some of
the complex political problems of our own time.

---

[1] See the Appendix to the first volume of Thucydides. The whole discussion as to the functions and influence of the τύραννοι and the relation between the aristocracy and the people, is very characteristic of the spirit in which Arnold gave historical lessons.

His pupils say that he was singularly successful in connecting the events recorded by Thucydides and Tacitus with parallel incidents in modern history. A discussion on the πέριοικοι of Athens — not exactly citizens, nor yet slaves — leads him to a comparison with the burghers of Augsburg, or with the unenfranchised commons of England. The steps by which the aristocracy of blood becomes in time overthrown by the aristocracy of wealth, and by which both may be in time superseded by the ascendency of mere numbers, he would illustrate in such a way as to show the fundamental likeness between some of the social and political problems of antiquity and those of our own day. Ancient and modern, he always contended, were misleading terms. For there was an ancient and a modern period in the history of every people. "And a large portion of that history which we are wont to call ancient, the later history of the Greek republics and that of the period of the Roman Empire, is practically modern, — much more modern, say, than the age of Alfred, as it describes society in a stage analogous to that which we have now reached in the history of England."[1]

This view of the essentially modern character of much of what is called ancient history, and of the practical identity of many of the social and political problems which present themselves for solution in different ages, is so important and so characteristic of Arnold's method that it needs to be more fully vindicated in his own words.

[1] Stanley, Chap. IV.

"The state of Greece from Pericles to Alexander, fully described to us as it is in the works of their great contemporary historians, poets, orators, and philosophers, affords a political lesson perhaps more applicable to our own times, if taken altogether, than any other portion of history which can be named anterior to the eighteenth century. When Thucydides, in his reflection on the bloody dissensions of Corcyra, notices the decay and extinction of the simplicity of old times, he marks the great transition from ancient history to modern, the transition from an age of feeling to one of reflection, from a period of ignorance and credulity to one of inquiry and scepticism. Now, such a transition took place in the sixteenth century; the period of the Reformation, when compared with the years preceding it, was undoubtedly one of inquiry and reflection. But still it was an age of strong feeling and of intense belief; the human mind cleared a space for itself within a certain circle, but except in individual cases, and even those scarcely avowed, there were still acknowledged limits of authority, which inquiry had not yet ventured to question. The period of Roman civilization from the time of the Gracchi to those of the Antonines was in this respect more completely modern, and, accordingly, this is one of the periods of history we should do well to study most carefully. In point of political experience we are, even at this hour, scarcely on a level with the statesmen of the age of Alexander. Mere lapse of years confers here no increase of knowledge; four thousand years have furnished the Asiatic with scarcely anything that deserves the name of political experience; two thousand years since the fall of Carthage have furnished the African with absolutely nothing. Even in Europe and in America it would not be easy now to collect such a treasure of experience as the constitutions of one hundred and fifty-three commonwealths along the various coasts of the Mediterranean offered to Aristotle. There he might study the institutions of various races derived from various sources: every possible variety of external position, of national character, of positive laws, agricultural and commercial, military powers and maritime, wealthy countries and poor ones, monarchies, aristocracies, and democracies, with every imaginable form and combination of each and all; states over-peopled and under-peopled, old and new, and in every circumstance of advance, maturity, and decline. Nor was the moral experience of the age of Greek civilization less complete. By moral experience I mean an acquaintance with the whole compass of these questions which relate to the metaphysical analysis of man's nature and faculties, and to the practical object of his being. This was derived from the strong, critical, and inquiring spirit of the Greek sophists and philosophers, and from the unbounded freedom which they enjoyed. In mere metaphysical research the schoolmen were indefatigable and bold, but in moral questions there was an authority which restrained them; among Christians the notions of duty and virtue must be assumed as beyond dispute. But not the wildest extravagance of atheistic wickedness in modern times can go further than the sophists of Greece went before them; whatever audacity can dare and subtilty contrive to make the words 'good' and 'evil' change their meaning has been already tried in the days of Plato, and by his eloquence and wisdom and faith unshaken has been put to shame. Thus it is that while the advance of civilization destroys much that was noble, and throws over the mass of human society an atmosphere somewhat dull and hard, yet it is only by its peculiar trials, no less than by its positive advantages, that the utmost virtue of human nature can be matured. And those who vainly lament that progress of earthly things, which, whether good or evil, is certainly inevitable, may be consoled by the thought that its sure tendency is to confirm and purify the virtue of the good; and that to us, holding in our hands not the wisdom of Plato only, but also a treasure of wisdom and of comfort which to Plato was denied, the utmost activity of the human mind may be viewed without apprehension, in the confidence that we possess a charm to deprive it of its evil, and to make it minister for ourselves certainly, and through us, if we use it rightly, for the world in general, to the more perfect triumph of God."[1]

In this long extract, it is evident that the object sought in the treatment of history as a school subject was not merely the conveyance of information or of useful knowledge. Indeed, Arnold thought that the favourite notion of filling a learner's memory with useful facts was likely to produce great mischief. "It was," he said, "a caricature of the principles of inductive philosophy which, while it taught the importance of a knowledge of facts, never imagined that this knowledge was of itself equivalent to wisdom." He proposed to begin with younger children by giving a few names of the greatest men of different periods, and by presenting to them pictures of historical scenes so as to form lasting associations with the most famous personages in history and the most remarkable actions in their lives. He would thus familiarize them with the poetry of history, the most striking characters and most heroic actions, whether of doing or suffering, but would abstain from embarrassing them with its philosophy, with the causes of revolutions, the progress of society, or the merits of great political questions.

"Biography would form an essential feature of such a course of lessons, partly as giving fixed points of human interest round which historical facts would cluster and adjust them-

[1] Preface to the third volume of Thucydides.

selves, and partly that in taking up any more detailed history or biography (and educators should never forget the importance of preparing a boy to derive benefit from his accidental reading), he may have some association with the subject of it, and may not feel himself on ground wholly unknown to him. Supposing that an outline of general history has thus been given to a boy by means of pictures and abridgements, that his associations, as far as they go, are strong and lively, and that a keen desire of knowledge has been awakened, the next thing to be done is to set him to read some first-rate historian whose mind was formed in some period of advanced civilization analogous to that in which we now live. Thus in time the learner may be introduced to that high philosophy which helps him "rerum cognoscere causas." Let him be taught to trace back institutions, civil and religious, to their origin, to explain the elements of the national character, as now exhibited in maturity, in the vicissitudes of a nation's fortune, and the moral and physical qualities of its race, to observe how the morals and the mind of the people have been subject to a succession of influences, some accidental, others regular, to see and remember what critical seasons of improvement have been neglected, what besetting evils have been wantonly aggravated by wickedness and folly. In short, the pupil may be furnished, as it were, with certain *formulæ* which shall enable him to read all history beneficially, shall teach him what to look for in it, how to judge of it, and how to apply it."

In all this we see an illustration of the intellectual process which Professor Laurie has called the deparochializing, of the student, the detachment of the mind from what is transitory in the politics of the present hour, to what is permanent and typical in the history of the human race.

"A man thus educated," Arnold argued, "even

though he knows no history in detail but that which is called ancient, will be far better fitted to enter on public life than he who could tell the circumstances and the date of every battle and of every debate throughout the last century, and whose information, in the common sense of the term, about modern history might be twenty times more minute. The fault of systems of classical education in some instances has been, not that they did not teach modern history, but that they did not prepare and dispose their pupils to acquaint themselves with it afterwards; not that they did not attempt to raise an impossible superstructure, but that they did not prepare the ground for the foundation and put the materials within reach of the builder. . . . It is no wisdom to make boys prodigies of information, but it is our wisdom and our duty to cultivate their faculties each in its season, first the memory and imagination, and then the judgment, to furnish them with the means, and to excite the desire of improving themselves, and to wait with confidence for God's blessing on the result."[1]

How early it was possible for a young and ingenuous mind to become impregnated with some of the Arnoldian enthusiasm may be judged from this passage in one of Arthur Stanley's letters to his sister, written three months after his admission to the school.

"We have been examined again by Dr. Arnold in Latin, and he seemed very much pleased with me. He is very par-

---

[1] Use of the Classics — Arnold's *Miscellaneous Works*, p. 359.

ticular. The least word you say or pronounce wrong he finds out in an instant, and he is very particular about chronology, history, and geography. He does not sit still like the other masters, but walks backwards and forwards all the time, and seems rather fidgety. Only a fortnight to Easter and the speeches. There are to be English verses. How I *shall* listen! . . . How particular he is, but at the same time so mild and pleasant. I like saying to him very much. He asks much about history, and puts queer, out-of-the-way questions. I daresay you will be glad to hear that I got up to the top place for answering something about Themistocles. He seems very much pleased when I answer anything."

The boy goes on to tell also how he has again seen Mrs. Arnold, and how "she talked to me about her children, and told me that little Matthew, the eldest of her boys, that morning had been in the garden, and got a red and white rose for her, and showing them to the Doctor, said, 'See, Papa, here are York and Lancaster.' It so happened that that very day the lesson with Dr. Arnold was history, and though there was nothing particular about it in the lesson, he asked a good deal about the devices of York and Lancaster. I daresay he was thinking about Matt and his roses."[1]

Incidentally, an interesting side light is thrown on his method of teaching by the method adopted in his Roman history. He had been profoundly impressed by the researches of Niebuhr into the earlier annals of Rome, and he regarded that writer as one who, by the method no less than by the results of his enqui-

[1] *Life of Dean Stanley*, Vol. I.

ries, had done for ancient history what Bacon did for science. Indeed, it may be said that this author's works exercised a singularly profound influence on Arnold's character, since they not only inspired him with new views of historical criticism, but by introducing him to German literature, opened out to him new realms of thought. With a view to make the result of Niebuhr's researches intelligible to English readers, he determined to set forth the legendary story of the first three centuries of the regal period of Rome in a manner likely to call special attention to its unhistorical and quasi-mythical character. Like all true teachers, he knew that truth of mere fact, — definite, verifiable truth, is not the only kind of truth worth studying. What actually happened about the beginnings of Rome, whether Æneas and Romulus ever lived, and what they did, are matters undoubtedly worth knowing if we can find them out. But what the Romans believed about the origin of their city is equally well worth knowing, for it helped to shape the polity of the Roman commonwealth, to form the national character, and to influence Roman literature. It is therefore as true a subject for the historian, and has exercised as great an influence on the fortunes and development of the human race as any dates and records which will satisfy the historical critic. It might be contended that the like argument would justify the historians of our own country in setting forth the legends of Brutus the Trojan, of Lear, and of Pendragon, as they are told by Geoffrey of Monmouth, Gildas, or Nennius, or later by Milton him-

self in his curious fragment of British history. But
it is manifest that the same reasons do not apply,
and that, interesting as these legends are, and fruitful
as they have been found by our poets, from Shakespeare to Tennyson, they have never been incorporated
in the popular belief, as the traditions of the prehistoric age of Rome had been. It was, however, very
characteristic of Arnold that he was unwilling to
dismiss these traditions as irrelevant and wholly
unhistorical, but that he sought rather to find for
them their due place in the narrative with a kind of
authenticity all their own. "I wished," he said in
his preface to the Roman history, "to give these
legends with the best effect, and at the same time
with a perpetual mark, not to be mistaken by the
most careless reader, that they were legends and not
history. There seemed a reason, therefore, for adopting a more antiquated style, which otherwise, of
course, would be justly liable to the charge of affectation." Most readers of his Roman history will be
ready to acknowledge that this aim has been well
fulfilled. The author has succeeded in adding a new
charm to the story of Romulus and Numa, and has
invested with the hues of poetry the beautiful legend
of the nymph Egeria, who "in her sacred grove and
by the spring that welled out of the rock taught the
good king all that he ought to do towards the gods
and towards men." It is pleasant thus to have the
old-world stories of the statesman-like Servius and
the wicked Tullia, the Sibylline books, the Delphic
oracle, and the expulsion of the Tarquins told with

simplicity in archaic and semi-Biblical language, while all the critical apparatus and discussion of their historical trustworthiness are appropriately reserved for separate treatment. One obtains, as this book is read, a glimpse of the method by which a teacher might vivify history and make it real and edifying to a nineteenth century learner, without robbing it of that *nuance* of poetry which makes the twilight of history so full of pathetic beauty.

And hence we are not surprised to learn that history as he treated it became a favourite subject with the boys. A schoolmaster who has no hobby, no subject which he teaches with special sympathy and with contagious enthusiasm, loses a great opportunity of influence. And it was soon perceived that his favourite books and periods the boys read zealously, and that his favourite heroes were theirs. The characters and thoughts of antiquity were to him and to them alike almost living and present. "A black cloud was on his brow when he spoke of Tiberius or Augustus or Napoleon, of the soulless Epicureanism of Horace or the coarseness of Juvenal; and few of his pupils have lost his enthusiasm for the often misrepresented and vilified Cicero, or for the best and holiest of kings, St. Louis of France. He denounced Polybius as a dull geographer and an overrated military historian, and Livy as a drunken helot, showing us what history ought not to be, and so uniformly careless as to make the Punic war as hard in the telling, as it was in the fighting." Thus, as Mr. Oscar Browning says:

F

"Arnold's deep interest in history, his grasp of all that was living and actual in the authors which he taught, were the springs of a literary stimulus, the effects of which frequently lasted through life. After reading St. Paul's denunciations of the sins of the heathen, he would turn to his Horace and say, 'Let us now see what this ancient world was like.'"

As an adjunct to history he attached special value to geography. The physical features of a country must be studied before the events which took place in it can be explained. As a topographical map is indispensable to the commander who undertakes a campaign, it is not less useful to one who wishes to understand the history of such a campaign. Carlyle did not undertake to describe the battle of Dunbar or of Rossbach until he had visited the spot and studied the conformation of the ground; and in like manner Arnold followed and traced with care the footsteps of Hannibal over the Alps. That Ostia in the time of Ancus Martius was at the mouth of the Tiber, though now seven miles from the sea, that Ravenna, in the time of Theodoric, was one of the most famous cities of Italy, though now, owing to the physical changes of the shore, an obscure and pestilential town, and that Rome itself owes its growth to its fortunate position in the midst of a large area of productive territory, were facts which seemed to him to have a significant bearing on the course of history.

"I have been working at Hannibal's passage of the Alps. How bad a geographer is Polybius, and how strange that he should be thought a good one! Compare him with any man who is really a geographer, — with Herodotus, with Napoleon, whose sketches of Italy, Egypt, and Syria, in his memoirs are unrivalled, — or with Niebuhr, and how striking is the difference. The dulness of Polybius' fancy made it impossible for him to conceive or paint scenery clearly, and how can a man be a geographer without lively images of the formation and features of the country which he describes? How different are the several Alpine valleys, and how would a few simple touches of the scenery which he seems actually to have visited, yet could neither understand nor feel it, have decided for ever the question of the route. *Now* the account suits no valley well, and therefore it may be applied to many; but I believe the real line was by the little St. Bernard, although I cannot trace the particular spots which De Luc and Cramer fancy they could recognise. I thought so on the spot (*i.e.*, that the route could not be traced) when I crossed the little St. Bernard with Polybius in my hand, and I think so still. How much we want a physical history of countries, tracing the changes they have undergone, either by such violent revolutions as volcanic phenomena, or by the slower but not less complete change produced by ordinary causes: such as alteration of climate occasioned by enclosing and draining, alteration in the course of rivers, and in the level of their beds, alteration in the animal and vegetable productions of the soil, and in the supply of metals and minerals, noting also the advance or retreat of the sea, and the origin and successive increase in the number and variation in the line of roads, together with the changes in the extent and character of the woodlands. How much might be done by our society at Rome if some of its attention were directed to these points; for instance, drainage and an alteration in the course of the waters have produced great changes in Tuscany, and there is also the interesting question as to the spread of malaria in the Maremma."[1]

[1] Letter CXII.

Dean Stanley gives another example of the way in which Arnold would vivify his lessons by associating geography and history.

"In the Seven Years' War he would illustrate the general connexion of military history with geography by the simple instance of the order of Hannibal's successive victories, and then chalking roughly on a board the chief points in the physical conformation of Germany, apply the same principle to the more complicated campaigns of Frederick the Great. Or again in a more general examination he would ask for the chief events which occurred, for instance, in the year 15, of two or three successive centuries, and by making the boys contrast or compare them together, bring before their minds the differences and resemblances in the state of Europe in each of the periods in question."

This passage is interesting as a revelation of one conspicuous note or characteristic of Arnold's teaching — its *thoroughness*. The truly effective teacher must not only know his subject or his text-book, he must look all round it, must survey from all sides the problem he has to solve and must furnish himself with such auxiliary information as may help him to illustrate the matter in hand from very different points of view. Arnold saw the necessity of widening the school curriculum, of giving to mathematics, modern languages, and even to rudimentary science increased attention and importance; but his own personal teaching was mainly confined, as we have seen, to divinity, language, literature, and to history, and to so much of geography as would make history and literature intelligible. Within that range nothing which had even an indirect bearing on the elucidation of the subject seemed to him unimportant or irrelevant. But outside this range, he habitually deferred to the judgment of others. When a boy brought him a question he was unable to answer, he would say frankly, "Go to Mr. Price," or perhaps some other assistant, "he knows more about it than I do." That affectation of omniscience which some teachers deem necessary for the maintenance of dignity seemed petty and unworthy in his eyes; and one of the lessons the boys learned from him was that one should have the courage to admit ignorance of many things, and that it was a mean thing to pretend to know that of which we are actually ignorant.

His views as to the right relation of a head master to his colleagues are well illustrated in these two extracts from letters, the first being one of enquiry for a master.

"What I want is a man who is a Christian and a gentleman — an active man, and one who has common sense and understands boys. I do not so much care about scholarship, as he will have immediately under him the lowest forms in the school; but yet, on second thoughts, I do care about it very much, because his pupils may be in the highest forms; and besides, I think that even the elements are best taught by a man who has a thorough knowledge of the matter. However, if one must give way, I prefer activity of mind, and an interest in his work, to high scholarship, for the one can be acquired more easily than the other."

In a letter addressed to a new master on his appointment, he amplifies this theme, and presents to us a picture of an ideal assistant.

"The qualifications which I deem essential to the due performance of a master's duties here may in brief be expressed as the spirit of a Christian and a gentleman — that a man should enter upon his business not ἐκ παρέργου, but as of substantive and most important duty; that he should devote himself to it as the especial branch of the ministerial calling which he has chosen to follow; that belonging to a great public institution, and sharing in a public and conspicuous situation, he should study things 'lovely and of good report'; that is, that he should be public-spirited, liberal, and entering heartily into the interest, honour, and general respectability and distinction of the society that he has joined, and that he should have sufficient vigour of mind, and thirst for knowledge, to persist in adding to his own stores, without neglecting the full improvement of those whom he is teaching. I think our masterships here offer a noble field of duty; and I would not bestow these on any one who I thought would undertake them without entering into the spirit of our system heart and hand."[1]

In short, his aim was first to surround himself with men worthy of trust, and then to trust them. Every three weeks a council was held, in which all school matters were discussed, and in which every one was free to express his opinion or propose any measure not in contradiction to any fundamental principle of school administration, and it not unfrequently happened that he himself was opposed and out-voted. He tried to strengthen the bonds which united the masters and the school, and their loyalty to one another, by offering in various ways means for friendly communication between them. He desired,

[1] Stanley, Chap. III.

also, that the masters should have "each a horse of his own to ride," independent of the mere phantasmagoria of boys passing successively through their respective forms. He had learned from experience how much his own mental horizon and his power of usefulness had been enlarged by the indulgence of intellectual hobbies not directly connected with the necessary routine of school work ; and when he discovered any special gift or taste on the part of a young master, he sought to find an opportunity for its exercise. A weak head master seeks to be an autocrat, and is fain to lay down mechanical rules with a view to secure that all his assistants shall conform to his pattern and his methods. It is only a strong man who can afford to encourage freedom and reasonable independence among his subordinates, and thus to secure their hearty co-operation. Yet without such freedom there will always be waste of power; the school will lack organic unity, and will fail to achieve its highest purposes.

Thus the ideal ever before the head master's mind was not that of a school in which it was the business of some to teach and others to learn, and in which the functions of the various members were clearly separated and defined, but an organized community for mutual help in the business both of teaching and learning. Education, he was wont to say, is not a mechanical but a dynamical process, and the more powerful and vigorous the mind of the teacher, the more clearly and readily he can grasp things, the better fitted he is to cultivate the mind of another.

"And to this I find myself coming more and more. I care less and less for information, more and more for the pure exercise of the mind, for answering a question concisely and comprehensively, for showing a command of language, delicacy of taste, a comprehensiveness of thought, and power of combination."[1]

The relations of a head master to a governing body are among the most difficult and delicate concernments of his life. The right of governors and trustees to control the general administration of the school and of its funds is undoubted; and deference, courtesy, and full information are their due from the master to whom they have confided the actual internal government of the school. But in Arnold's view the delimitation of power and responsibility should be very clearly marked. Fuller has said of the good schoolmaster, that "he is and will be known to be an absolute monarch in his school." And this is indeed the only condition on which a high-minded man, conscious of power and of a clear purpose, could accept a head-mastership. The trustees have always their remedy. They may dismiss, without assigning cause, a master in whom, for any reason, they have ceased to have confidence. But until they do so, his authority is absolute. While seeking, therefore, to cultivate the most friendly relations with the trustees, Arnold was very resolute in regard to the rights and privileges of his office. And when on the appearance of an article in the *Edinburgh Review*, which was generally and rightly attributed to him, an influential

[1] Letter CXXIV.

governor of the school wrote to ask him if he were the author, he replied without hesitation. The letters following have in fact established a precedent of which many later teachers have availed themselves for their own protection against interference within the sphere of their own lawful freedom and responsibility. Earl Howe wrote to him requesting, as one of the trustees of Rugby School, that Dr. Arnold would declare if he was the author of the article on Dr. Hampden in the *Edinburgh Review*, and stating that his conduct would be guided by Dr. Arnold's answer.

"RUGBY, June 22, 1836.

"MY LORD, —

"The answer which your Lordship has asked for I have given several times to many of my friends; and I am well known to be very little apt to disavow or conceal my authorship of anything that I may at any time have written. Still, as I conceive your Lordship's question to be one which none but a personal friend has the slightest right to put to me, or to any man, I feel it due to myself to decline giving any answer to it."

In reply to a second letter in which Lord Howe urged compliance with his request, on the grounds that he might feel constrained by official duty to take some step in the matter in case the report were true, Arnold says:

"Your Lordship addressed me in a tone purely formal and official, and at the same time asked a question which the common usage of society regards as one of delicacy — justified I do not say, only by personal friendship, but at least by some familiarity of acquaintance. It was because no such ground could exist in the present case, and because I cannot and do not acknowledge your right officially as a trustee of Rugby School, to question me on the subject of my real or supposed writings on matters wholly unconnected with the school, that I felt it my duty to decline answering your Lordship's question.

"It is very painful to be placed in a situation where I must either appear to seek concealment wholly foreign to my wishes, or else must acknowledge a right which I owe it, not only to myself, but to the master of every endowed school in England, absolutely to deny. But in the present case, I think I can hardly be suspected of seeking concealment. I have spoken on the subject of the article in the *Edinburgh Review*, freely, in the hearing of many, with no request for secrecy, on their part, expressed or implied. Officially, however, I cannot return an answer, not from the slightest feeling of disrespect to your Lordship, but because my answering would allow a principle which I can, on no account, admit to be just or reasonable."

CHAPTER V

Arnold as a disciplinarian — Moral evils in school — Description of their danger — Mr. Welldon's picture of school life — Fagging — Luxury and idleness — Expulsion — Religious lessons — Chapel services — School sermons — Extravagance — Home influence — Mental cultivation a religious duty — A memorable sermon — Religious exercises — Corporate life of a great school — What is Christian education — Clerical schoolmasters — The influence of Arnold's sermons generally — Punishments — Study of individual character — Games and athletics — *Tom Brown's School Days* — Rugby boys at the Universities — Bishop Percival's estimate

ARNOLD'S fame, however, rests more largely on his work as a ruler and administrator, than on his special gifts as a teacher. It was the discipline, the $\mathring{\eta}\theta o\varsigma$, the moral atmosphere of Rugby, on which, as he himself desired, his influence was most strongly felt. He had from the first an oppressive sense of the formidable character of the task he had undertaken; of the vast capacity for evil which lay yet undeveloped in a crowd of young, high-spirited, lawless lads; and yet of the boundless possibilities of good which were there also. "The management of boys," he said, "has all the interest of a great game of chess with living creatures for pawns and pieces, and your adversary in plain English the devil, who truly plays a tough game and is very hard to beat." It is a familiar fact in the experience of teachers that the interval between childhood and manhood is a somewhat intractable period; — a state of transition wherein the several elements of our composite nature exist for the time in unfavourable proportions. The shepherd's wish in the *Winter's Tale*, "I would there were no age between ten and three and twenty, or that youth would sleep out the rest," has found an echo in the thoughts of many a schoolmaster. Boys, however, decline to go to sleep from ten years old till twenty-three. They are in fact very much alive, and Arnold was sometimes appalled at the task he had undertaken. When he went to Rugby, the state of morals and behaviour was eminently disheartening; drunkenness and swearing were common vices; a reckless defiance of authority, and a hatred of submission to it, were combined with a servile cringing to the public opinion of the school. There was great readiness to combine for evil, and a systematic persecution carried on by the bad against the good. Dr. Moberly, head master of Winchester, and afterwards Bishop of Salisbury, says that "the tone of young men who came up to the University from Winchester, Eton, Rugby, or Harrow, was universally irreligious. A religious undergraduate was very rare, and was much laughed at when he appeared."

An outspoken passage from one of Arnold's school sermons shows how true a diagnosis he had made of the evils he had to encounter, and how deep was his sense of the dangers and pitfalls which surround life in a great public school.

"What the aspect of public schools is when viewed with a Christian eye, and what are the feelings with which men who do not really turn to God in after life look back upon their years passed at school, I cannot express better than in the words of one[1] who had himself been at a public school, who afterwards became a most exemplary Christian, and who in what I am going to quote seems to describe his own experience. 'Public schools,' he says, 'are the very seats and nurseries of vice. It may be unavoidable, or it may not, but the fact is indisputable. None can pass through a large school without being pretty intimately acquainted with vice, and few, alas! very few, without tasting too largely of that poisoned bowl. The hour of grace and repentance at length arrives, and they are astonished at their former fatuity. . . .'

"I am afraid," Arnold goes on to say, "that the fact is indeed indisputable. Public schools *are* the very seats and nurseries of vice. But the same writer says further, 'It may be unavoidable, or it may not,' and these words seem to me as though they ought to fill us with the deepest shame of all. For what a notion does it give that we should have been so long and constantly bad that it may be doubted whether our badness be not unavoidable, whether we are not evil hopelessly and incurably. And this to be true of places which were intended to be seats of Christian education, and in all of which, I believe, the same words are used in the daily prayers which we use regularly here! God is thanked for those founders and benefactors by whose benefits the whole school is brought up to godliness and good learning! . . . What is meant when public schools are called 'the seats and nurseries of vice'? That is properly a nursery of vice where a boy unlearns the pure and honest principles which he may have received at home, and gets in their stead others which are utterly low and base and mischievous, where he loses his modesty, his respect for truth, and his affectionateness, and becomes coarse and false and unfeeling. That, too, is a nursery of vice, and most fearfully so, where vice is bold and forward and presuming, and goodness is

[1] Mr. John Bowdler, *Remains*, Vol. II., p. 153.

timid and shy, and exists as if by sufferance; where the good, instead of setting the tone of society and branding with disgrace those who disregard it, are themselves exposed to reproach for their goodness, and shrink before the open avowal of evil principles which the bad are striving to make the law of the community. That is a nursery of vice where the restraints laid upon evil are considered as so much taken from liberty, and where, generally speaking, evil is more willingly screened and concealed than detected and punished. What society would be if men regarded the laws of God and man as a grievance, and thought liberty consisted in following to the full their proud and selfish and low inclinations, that schools to a great extent are, and therefore they may be well called 'the seats and nurseries of vice.'"[1]

The peculiar conditions which help to determine the public opinion of a great school have been described with much vividness and clearness of insight, by a later head master of large and varied experience.

"The modern bed of Procrustes, is, or was, a public school. Nowhere in the world is there so keen an appreciation of those who adapt themselves to local tone, temper, and custom. But nowhere is departure, however slight, from the recognized standard of propriety visited with consequences so unfailing. The society of a public school is a world in itself, self-centred, self-satisfied. It takes but slight account of the principles and practices which obtain in the world of men. It has its own laws, its own fashions, its own accepted code of morals. To these all persons must submit, or the penalty of resistance is heavy. Its virtues are not altogether those of men and women, nor are its vices. Some actions of which the world thinks comparatively little, it honours with profound admiration. To

[1] Sermon XII., Vol. 2.

others which the world thinks much of, it is indifferent. There, physical courage, for instance, is esteemed too highly. Self-repression is depreciated. Hypocrisy is loathed. But the inverted hypocrisy — the homage which virtue pays to vice — or, in other words, the affectation of being worse than one really is, is common among boys, and is thought to be honourable. Truth, again, is not esteemed as a virtue of universal application, but is relative to particular persons, a falsehood, if told to a schoolfellow, being worse than if told to a master. Nobody can be intimate with a community of schoolboys and not feel that a morality so absolute, yet so narrow, and in some ways so perverted, bears a certain resemblance to the morality of a savage tribe. It is rather the germ of morals, than morality itself. . . . What may be called the uncivilized or unsoftened spirit in public school life is seen in the homage paid among public-school boys to physical faculties and performances. Of the achievements of the intellect, if they stand alone, public-school opinion is still, as it has always been, slightly contemptuous. But strength, speed, athletic skill, quickness of eye and hand, still command universal applause among schoolboys, as among savages." [1]

How Arnold sought to meet the difficulties of the task before him, and by what expedients he endeavoured to clear the moral atmosphere of the school, and to set up by degrees a higher standard both of aim and achievement in school-boy life, cannot be fully understood without acquaintance with the fuller details which are given in Stanley's *Life*. It may suffice here to enumerate them briefly. The steps he took in the way of reform were, even when boldest and most resolute, cautious and tentative. He had the wisdom to

[1] *Gerald Eversley's Friendship*, J. E. C. Welldon, p. 75.

know that a new head master who insists at once on measures of reform which appear to his colleagues and to the older boys to be needless and revolutionary, may defeat his own purpose by creating the friction and opposition a little tact might render unnecessary. His first duty is to accept and turn to use whatever of good there is in the existing system, his next to modify and improve that system, as experience enables him to make sure of his ground. For example, he made no attempt to abolish fagging, but determined to avail himself of that venerable institution. "Another system," he said, "might perhaps be better than this, but I am placed here in the midst of this one and must make the best of it." So he first sought and won the confidence of the sixth form, told them frankly that he regarded them as invested with responsibility, and that he relied on their help. "I want you to feel," he used to say to them, "how enormous is the influence you possess here on all below you." Nothing seemed to him of so much importance as to secure a body of præpostors distinguished by high principle, gentlemanly conduct, and intellectual ability. "You should feel," he told them, "like officers in the army whose want of moral courage would be thought cowardice. When I have confidence in the sixth, there is no post in England for which I would exchange this; but if they do not support me, I must go." He believed that one way of making a boy a gentleman was to treat him as one, and to show that he was respected and trusted. Even in the lower part of the school he never seemed on the watch for boys, and in the higher any attempt at further proof of an assertion was at once checked. "If you say so, that is quite enough for me; of course I take your word." And hence it came to be the current opinion of the school that it was a shame to tell Arnold a lie, for he always believed it!

The annals of English education present to our view no eminent teacher who was more profoundly penetrated than Arnold with the need of a moral basis for all school work. Aristotle had taught him that in advancing towards ideal perfection, the improvement of the moral faculties should go on concurrently with the development of intellectual powers. Hence he never ceased to insist on the paramount importance of training as distinguished from teaching. Every evil habit conquered, and every good habit formed, he knew would remove one obstacle to the energy of the intellect and assist in invigorating its nature. He thought that few spectacles were more appalling than that of a youth of high mental gifts divorced from moral principle.

When habits of self-indulgence and lawlessness have become so confirmed in a community of high-spirited youths as to be part of its traditions, rapid and drastic reform is practically impossible, and it would be dangerous and Quixotic for a master to attempt it. It was therefore by degrees that Arnold sought to remove the worst and most obstinate of these usages. For example, the practice of keeping beagles and guns surreptitiously in the back premises of the boarding-houses was effectually stopped, not by a peremptory prohibition, but by simply ruling that houses in which they were kept should be held to be out of the school bounds,— a rule which practically involved something like financial ruin to the house-master unless a change were made. It was more difficult to deal with the sporting section of the elder boys, who were wont to hire horses at Dunchurch, three miles off, in the heart of a famous hunting country, and to indulge in steeplechase and other races. Mr. Hughes tells of one such race which excited so much animation and enthusiasm among the boys that they resolved to have another, and made all arrangements with jockeys and umpires for a longer race across country. It was commonly said of Arnold that he knew better than any one when to look, and when to see nothing. However, it was expected in this case that there would be a "row," and that he would publicly notice the breach of rule which had been committed, and forbid its intended repetition. Nothing, however, was publicly said; but in the evening the chief of the sportsmen, a promising sixth-form youth, was sent for, and the Doctor said: "I know all about the match you rode the other day. If I had taken any public notice of it, I must have expelled you publicly. This would have ruined your career at Oxford, where you have just matriculated, and I hope will do well. But I have written to your father to tell him of your flagrant breach of discipline. And now let me warn you and your friends. I know what you are intending, and I will expel every boy who rides or is present, and will have the road watched to get the names." Mr. Hughes adds, "That race did not come off, or any other during Arnold's time." That boys should wish to *see* a race he thought reasonable enough; and a few weeks afterwards, when there was a grand steeplechase at Dunchurch, we find Clough writing to Arthur Stanley, "Arnold very wisely and indulgently altered the hour of calling over, and took off the Dunchurch prohibition for the day, so at least nine-tenths of the school were present to see the sport."[1]

Again, he resolutely expelled a boy whose influence tended to degrade the public opinion of the school or to be seriously detrimental to his companions. There were few points on which he was more emphatic and determined than this. "Undoubtedly it would be better if there was no evil, but evil being unavoidable, we are not a jail to keep it in, but a place of education where we must cast it out, to prevent its taint from spreading." Again, "If a boy has set his mind to do nothing, but considers all the work here as so much fudge, which he will evade if he can, he is sure to corrupt the rest, and I will send him away without scruple." Such a course necessarily proved unpopular, and brought about at first a good deal of remonstrance from parents and muttered discontent among the boys. They were scared and silenced, however, when he broke out one day with the oft-quoted allocution: "It is not necessary that this should be a school for three hundred, or even one

[1] *The Great Public Schools.* Article on Rugby.

hundred, boys, but it *is* necessary that it should be a school of Christian gentlemen." Those who have seen in the National Portrait Gallery in London the admirable portrait of Arnold by Phillips, and have marked the keen eye, the firm and resolute mouth, and the masterful pose of the head will easily understand the tone in which he would utter these words and the rather startling effect which they produced.

Yet it is noticeable that although his great aim was to give a Christian tone to the little community, he did not set about increasing the number of religious services or theological lessons, or rely for the fulfilment of his ideal on what is often described as definite dogmatic teaching. "He shrank," says Stanley, "from pressing on the conscience of boys rules of action which he felt they were not yet able to bear, and from enforcing acts which, though right in themselves, would in boys be performed from wrong motives."

The school chapel became, under Arnold's régime, the centre of the religious life of the community, and played an important part in the discipline of the school. Before his time there had been a chaplain at Rugby as well as a head master, but three years after Arnold's appointment the former office fell vacant, and he applied to the trustees for the appointment without the salary. The use he made of his new office will be fully appreciated by all who read the published volumes containing the sermons preached in Rugby chapel. Arthur Stanley, at the age of eighteen, said of Arnold's sermons that he never heard or saw anything which gave him so strongly the idea of inspiration. The prevailing note of these sermons is intense seriousness,—a deep sense both of the need of a high ideal in life and of the difficulties which attend its realization. His conception of the purpose which a school sermon ought to serve is well illustrated in this passage:

"It is not enough to speak of sin in general and holiness in general, of God and Christ, of death and judgement. Something more clear and distinct is wanted. You know very well that your faults are not those which you read of most in books, for books are written by men, and in general are intended to be read by men; they speak therefore mostly of the sins and temptations of manhood: of covetousness, ambition, injustice, pride, and other older vices with which you feel that you have as yet but small concern. Besides, the pulpit is a solemn and sacred place, whereas the matters with which you are daily engaged are so common and so humble, that it seems like a want of reverence to speak of them in a sermon plainly by their names. And yet, if we do not speak of them plainly by their names, half of what we say will be lost in the air."[1]

Accordingly, we find throughout the sermons evidence of a full acquaintance with the peculiar temptations which school life presents, and a keen insight into the effects produced by them upon the character. Perhaps of all the evils he denounced and sought to expose, the worst was the cowardice which made boys succumb to the public opinion of the set in which they happened to live.

[1] Sermon V., Vol. II.

"There are boys who have either never learned, or have quite forgotten all that may have been told them at home, of the duty of attending to their school lessons. We know that there are boys who think all their lessons merely tiresome, and who are resolved never to take any more trouble about them than they can possibly avoid. But being thus idle themselves they cannot bear that others should be more attentive. We all know the terms of reproach and ridicule which are thrown out against a boy who works in earnest and upon principle. He is laughed at for taking unnecessary trouble, for being afraid of punishment, or for wishing to gain favour with his masters, and be thought by them to be better than other boys. Either of these reproaches is one which a boy finds it very hard to bear; he does not like to be thought afraid, or as wishing to court favour. He has not age or sense or firmness enough to know, that the only fear of which he needs be ashamed is the fear of his equals, the fear of those who are in no respect better than himself, and have, therefore, no right to direct him. To be afraid then of other boys is, in a boy, the same sort of weakness as it is in a man to be afraid of other men, and as a man ought to be equally ashamed of fearing men and of not fearing God, so a boy ought to be ashamed of fearing boys, and also to be ashamed of not fearing his parents and instructors. And as in after life, the fear of God makes no man do anything mean or dishonourable, but the fear of men does lead to all sorts of weakness and baseness, so among boys the fear of their parents and teachers will only make them manly and noble and high-spirited, but the fear of their companions leads them to be everything low and childish and contemptible."

Another common school vice, that of extravagance, he traced with pitiless clearness to its root in moral cowardice:

"There are some boys who, remembering the wishes of their parents, are extremely unwilling to incur debts and to spend a great deal of money upon their own eating, drinking, and amusements. There are some, too, who, knowing that the use of wine or any liquor of that sort is forbidden, because the use of it among boys is sure to be the abuse of it, would not indulge in anything of the kind themselves. But they are assailed by the example and the reproaches and the laughter of others. It is mean and poor-spirited and ungenerous not to contribute to the pleasures and social enjoyments of their companions; in short, not to do as others do. The charge of stinginess, of not spending his money liberally, is one which a boy is particularly sore at hearing. He forgets that in his case such a charge is the greatest possible folly. Where is the generosity of spending money which is not your own, and which, as soon as it is spent, is to be supplied again with no sacrifice on your part? Where is the stinginess of not choosing to beg money of your dearest friends in order to employ it in a manner which those friends would disapprove? For after all the money must come from them, as you have it not, nor can you earn it for yourselves. But there is another laugh behind; a boy is laughed at for being kept so strictly at home that he cannot get money as he likes, and he is taught to feel ashamed and angry at the hard restraint which is laid upon him. Truly that boy has gone a good way in the devil's service, who will dare to set another against his father and mother, and who will teach him that their care and authority are things which he should be ashamed of."[1]

His perception of the evils and dangers which attended public-school life will thus be seen to have been very keen, yet his biographer tells us that there was hardly ever a sermon which did not contain some

[1] Sermon VIII., p. 71.

words of encouragement. "I have never," he said in his last sermon, "wished to speak with exaggeration; it seems to me as unwise as it is wrong to do so. I think that it is quite right to observe what is hopeful in us as well as what is threatening. General confessions of unmixed evils are deceiving and hardening rather than arousing, and our evil never looks so really dark as when we contrast it with anything which there may be in us of good."[1]

Although by his own early training, and by the necessities of his position as head master of Rugby, he was essentially a "public-school" man, identified with the system of great boarding-schools, he was not insensible to the disadvantages of that system, not the least of which was the alienation of the boys from home influence. In his view the ideal method of education was a combination of the home and the school, and he thought it a misfortune to a boy to be handed over for so large a portion of his young life to the care of strangers, in an artificial community, in which the domestic affections, which ought ever to exercise so large a share in the formation of a noble character, were necessarily overlaid or discouraged.

"You sometimes," he said, "learn to feel ashamed of indulging your natural affections, and particularly of being attached to your mothers and sisters, and fond of their society. You fancy it is unmanly to be thought to have been influenced by them, and you are afraid of being supposed to long too much for their tenderness and indulgent

---

[1] *Sermons*, Vol. V., p. 460.

kindness towards you. . . . I am afraid, it cannot be doubted, that it is peculiarly the effect of the public schools of England to lower and weaken the connexion between parent and child, to lessen mutual confidence, and to make a son regard his father with more of respect than of love. Certainly, at least, the relation in other countries of Europe is on a different footing; there is more of cordial intimacy, more of real familiar friendship between parents and children than generally exists among us. . . . The situation of those boys I have always thought most fortunate, with all the opportunities of forming lasting friendships with those of their own age, which a public school so largely affords, and with the opportunities also of keeping up all their home affections, of never losing that lively interest in all that is said and done under their father's roof, which an absence of several months cannot fail in some measure to chill. . . . Your fault then is by so much the greater if you make yourselves strangers to domestic feelings and affections; if you think you have any dearer friendships, or any that can better become youth or manhood, than those which God himself has marked out for you in your homes. Add others to them if you will, and it is your duty and your wisdom to do so. . . . But beware how you let any less sacred connexion weaken the solemn and universal bond of domestic love. Remember that when Christ took our nature upon Him and went through every stage of human life to show us our peculiar duties in each, one of the only two things recorded of Him before He arrived at manhood, is His dutiful regard to His parents. 'He went down to Nazareth and was subject unto them.'"

One important feature of his preaching was the constant insistence on mental cultivation as a religious duty. It is difficult to measure the harm which is done by some religious teachers in speaking of the cultivation of the intellect as a thing apart from the religious life. It is far more common to hear from pulpits denunciations of the pride of intellect and the dangers of secular learning, than to receive a serious exhortation to make the best of our intellectual powers, and so to fit ourselves better for the possession of influence and for the discharge of duty. But to Arnold it always appeared that the religion of a school-boy should include diligence and study, and a sedulous cultivation of whatever powers and gifts he might possess.

"Generally, to all young persons God's call is to improve themselves, but what particular sort of improvement he calls you to, may be learned from the station of life in which he has placed you. If you were born in a station in which you would be called upon to work chiefly with your hands hereafter, then the strengthening of your bodies, the learning to be active and handy, to be bold and enduring of bodily pain and labour, would be your special duty over and above the common duty of love to God and man, which belongs to every age and every condition alike. . . . Although it be very true that the mind works feebly when the body is sickly, and that therefore you are called upon like all other persons, to make yourselves, as far as you can, strong and active and healthful and patient in your bodies, yet your especial call is rather to improve your minds, because it is with your minds that God calls upon you to work hereafter."[1]

The same view is strongly accentuated in a letter to an old pupil. "I rejoice that your mind seems to be in a healthier state about the prosecution of your studies. I am quite sure that it is a most solemn

[1] Sermon XIII.

duty to cultivate our understandings to the uttermost, for I have seen the evil moral consequences of fanaticism to a greater degree than I ever expected to see them realized, and I am satisfied that a neglected intellect is far oftener the cause of mischief to a man than a perverted or overvalued one."[1]

It will be observed that throughout the school sermons there is much less of theological teaching than of an endeavour to illustrate the bearing of Christianity on the daily practical life of the school-boy. The love of truth, the love of home, the conditions of honest intellectual work, and the responsibility which rests upon the possessors either of knowledge or of other gifts to make those gifts of service to others, are the constant themes. Arnold's dread of unreality made him shrink from any attempt to set before the boys impossible standards, or to exact from them language implying maturer convictions than it was possible for them to possess. He dreaded most of all unreality, or insincere professions of religion. He was not at all distinguished for the use of current religious phraseology in his intercourse with boys; still less was he willing to encourage them to employ such phraseology to him or to one another. He believed that would be beginning at the wrong end. If in time he made religious services and lessons more prominent, it was by slow degrees that he first sought to create the wish for them as privileges, rather than to impose them by authority as duties. For example, he took advantage of the awe and seriousness which

[1] Stanley, Letter CXXXVIII.

came over the whole community when one of the boys died; and on the following day, which was Sunday, he said:

"When I came yesterday from visiting the death-bed of him who has been taken from us, and looked round upon all the familiar objects and scenes within our own ground, — where your common amusements were going on, with your common cheerfulness and activity, — I felt that there was nothing painful in that; it did not seem in any way shocking, or out of tune with those feelings which the sight of a dying Christian must be supposed to awaken. The unsuitableness in point of natural feeling between scenes of mourning and scenes of liveliness did not at all present itself. But I did feel that if any of those faults had been brought before me which sometimes occur amongst us, had I heard that any of you had been guilty of falsehood or drunkenness, or any such sin, had I heard from any quarter the language of profaneness or unkindness or indecency, had I heard or seen any signs of that wretched folly which courts the laugh of fools by affecting to dread evil and not to care for good, then the unsuitableness of any of these things with the scene I had just quitted would have been intensely painful. And why? Not because such things would really have been worse than at any other time, but because at such a moment the eyes are opened really to know good and evil; because we then feel what it is so to live that death becomes an infinite blessing, and also what it is so to live that it were good for us if we had never been born."

It was at this time that he introduced into the sixth form the habit of using a short prayer before the first exercise every day, over and above the ordinary morning prayers. He did not attempt this in the lower part of the school; younger boys were not prepared to appreciate or welcome such an innovation; but when he had conveyed into the minds of his highest class the conviction that every-day work ought to be consecrated, and that the contrast between a death-bed scene and the routine of school business ought not to be painful, and would not be so if the school business itself were made religious, it will be seen that the daily prayer before the first lesson had a new meaning; for here the outward religious form came *after* the feeling which it was meant to express, and not before it or apart from it.

Arnold had great faith in the educative and ennobling influence of association with a *great* school, as distinguished from a small or private seminary. He knew that for a youth on entering into life it was a high privilege to belong to an institution or a society with great and venerable traditions and a long historic record, — a society of which he was proud, and which he might reasonably hope would some day become proud of him. He had learned from his master Aristotle that, though private education might be useful in special cases to correct particular faults, yet that in the main, education in public institutions watched over, if not prescribed, by the State, was the best fitted to prepare a man for the duties of citizenship and for the work of life. The noble conception of Aristotle of the magnanimous man, his scorn of the μικρόψυχος, or small-souled man, were ever present to Arnold's mind, and he thought a scholar was in part protected from littleness by belonging to a community which had large and far-reaching interests and was recognized by the State as a public institution. Hence he never ceased to dwell on the importance of sustaining the corporate life and the feeling of corporate interests in the school. In a sermon preached at Rugby on Founder's day, this view is stated at length with much clearness and force:

"It seems to me that there is, or ought to be, something very ennobling in being connected with any establishment at once ancient and magnificent, where all about us and all the associations belonging to the objects around us should be great, splendid, and elevating. What an individual ought to derive, and often does derive, from the feeling that he is born of an old and illustrious race, from being familiar from his childhood with the walls and with the trees that speak of the past no less than of the present, and make both full of images of greatness, this in an inferior degree belongs to every member of an ancient and celebrated place of education. In this respect every one has a responsibility imposed upon him, which I wish that we more considered. We know how school traditions are handed down from one school generation to another, and what is it, if in all these there shall be nothing great, nothing distinguished, nothing but a record, to say the best of it, of mere boyish amusements, when it is not a record of boyish follies? Every generation in which a low and foolish spirit prevails does its best to pollute the local influences of the place, to deprive the thought of belonging to it of anything that may enkindle and ennoble the minds of those who come after it. And if these foolish or tame associations continue, they make the evil worse; persons who appreciate highly the elevating influence of a great and ancient foundation will no longer send their sons to a place which has forfeited one of its most valuable powers, whose antiquity has nothing of the dignity, nothing of the romance, of antiquity, but is either a blank or worse than a blank. So the spirit gets lower and lower, and instead of finding a help and an encouragement in the associations of its place of education, the ingenuous mind feels them all no more than a weight upon its efforts; they only tend to thwart it and keep it down. This is the tendency not only of a vicious tone, but even of a foolish and childish one, of a tone that tolerates ignorance and an indifference about all save the amusements of the day. On the other hand, whatever is done here well and honourably, outlives its own generation. . . . The size, the scale, the wealth, of a great institution like this ensures its permanency, so far as anything on earth is permanent. The good and the evil, the nobleness or the vileness, which may exist on this ground now, will live and breathe here in the days of our children; they will form the atmosphere in which they will live hereafter, either wholesome and invigorating, or numbing and deadly."[1]

Arnold's dread of any theory which would tend to view the life of the scholar as a thing apart from the life of a Christian, found further expression in a memorable sermon on Christian education, from the striking text in Deuteronomy, "Ye shall teach these my words unto your children, speaking of them when thou sittest in thine house and when thou walkest by the way, when thou liest down, and when thou risest up." The preacher takes the opportunity of protesting earnestly against any attempt to divorce religious from secular instruction, or to treat them as distinct parts of an educational scheme. The device sometimes advocated in later times for solving the religious difficulty in our common and municipal schools, by confining the functions of the school

[1] Sermon XVI., Vol. III., p. 210.

teacher to secular instruction and calling in the aid of the clergy or other specialists to give lessons on religion at separate hours, would have seemed to him wholly indefensible, and indeed fatal to any true conception of the relation of religious knowledge to other knowledge.

"It is clear that neither is the Bible alone sufficient to give a complete religious education, nor is it possible to teach history, and moral and political philosophy, with no reference to the Bible, without giving an education that shall be antireligious. For, in the one case, the rule is given without the application, and in the other, the application is derived from a wrong rule. If, indeed, history were rigorously nothing but a simple collection of particular facts; if the writers made no remarks on them, and the readers drew from them no conclusions, there might indeed be no reference to a wrong rule, and the study might be harmless except as a waste of time. But as this is not and cannot be the case, as almost every writer of history does comment upon his facts and reason about them, and as all readers, even when they cannot be said to draw conclusions from a history, are yet sure to catch some moral impression, so it becomes impossible to read and think much about human actions and human character, without referring both to God's standard, and yet, at the same time, to avoid separating off a large portion of our moral nature from the guidance and habitual sovereignty of God."[1]

His strongest sentiment as a teacher, that the intellectual life should be dominated and controlled by moral and spiritual influences, is well summed up in a phrase which occurs in a letter to an old pupil. "I call by the name of wisdom, knowledge rich and

[1] Sermon XVI., Vol. III.

varied, digested and combined, and pervaded through and through by the light of the spirit of God."

The union of the clerical office with that of the schoolmaster, which, with few exceptions, has been the traditional practice of the public schools for four centuries, was thus in Arnold's case justified in a remarkable degree. And there can be no doubt that it has some advantages. Parents, in parting with the moral supervision of their sons, are not unreasonably disposed to place increased confidence in a head master who combines the scholarship and skill of the teacher with the dignity and weight of the clergyman's office. And it is unquestionable that the opportunity thus afforded to the head master of performing pastoral functions, and especially of preaching in the school chapel, gives unity to the whole discipline of the institution and adds to his own means of influence. In days in which scholars by profession were nearly all in holy orders, the most obvious and reasonable course for a governing body was to choose the head master from the clerical ranks. But in view of the state of learning and the educational requirements of our own times, the survival of this usage is not only undesirable, but often mischievous. It seriously narrows the range of choice open to trustees and governors. Many men of the highest academic distinction do not take orders, and yet desire to devote themselves to the profession of teacher. The demand for skill and educational experience, in addition to some acquaintance with the philosophy and the history of teach-

H

ing, is daily more audible; and experience does not show that these qualities are more likely to be possessed by a clergyman than by a layman. The fact that the head-mastership of a great public school often proves a step to ecclesiastical preferment is in itself not without its drawbacks. It subordinates the profession of a teacher to that of a church dignitary; it prevents the bestowal of a man's best powers upon the duties of a schoolmaster, by setting before him as an object of higher ambition the attainment of a deanery or a bishopric. Sometimes, also, the candidate for the headship of a public school expresses his willingness to take orders if he is elected; although, teaching apart, the clerical vocation may not be specially congenial to him. In this way a grave injustice is often done to scholars of eminence, who have sought to qualify themselves for the profession of teaching and intend to make it the business of their lives.

We may look forward, then, with hope to the time when, as a rule, laymen will fill the highest scholastic offices, or when, at least, men will be chosen for those offices on the grounds of their professional qualifications only, without reference to the accident of their having taken or not taken holy orders. In no other way can the function of the schoolmaster assume its rightful rank among the liberal and learned professions. Nevertheless, it will nearly always happen that a person gifted with the true teaching instinct, and conscious of his own responsibility in regard to the moral and spiritual well-being of his scholars, will greatly value the opportunity of addressing the school collectively on the highest of all subjects. And for this purpose a license to preach in the college chapel should be obtained from the bishop of the diocese. No breach of church order would occur if the school were thus regarded as a *peculium*, outside the ordinary ecclesiastical rules, with its ordained chaplain for the performance of the Church's ordinances, and with special recognition of the right of the head master to address the whole community from the pulpit whenever he desired to do so.

Of Arnold's sermons we may say generally that they do not aim at theological teaching, and that there is a marked absence of what is often called dogmatic statement, or of any attempt prematurely to form the *opinions* of boys on disputable religious questions.

"Give me credit," he says in a letter to a friend, "for a most sincere desire to make Rugby a place of Christian education. At the same time my object will be, if possible, to form Christian men, for Christian boys I can scarcely hope to make. I mean that, from the naturally imperfect state of boyhood, they are not susceptible of Christian principles in their full development and practice; and I suspect that a low standard of morals in many respects must be tolerated among them, as it was on a larger scale, in what I consider the boyhood of the human race."

Hence we trace throughout the school sermons an effort to awaken and inform the conscience, to arouse reverence for sacred things, and, above all, for the character and example of Christ; to inculcate the habit of veracity and the love of truth for its own sake, rather than to enforce any number of *truths* as understood by theologians; and to encourage diligence in the discharge of school duty, and right and generous aspirations after future honour and usefulness. As the best means of attaining these ends, he always extolled the virtue of that courage which will resist what is evil in the public opinion of the school, and which will render all other forms of excellence easier and more possible. Nearly all boyish faults and vices he knew ultimately resolved themselves into cowardice. Falsehood, indolence, shirking, the low ideal of duty which comes from acquiescence in the worst usages of one's fellows,— all were traceable to lack of courage. *L'esprit de solidarité dans le mal*, he thought the most dangerous of a school-boy's temptations, and he never ceased to expose it and to denounce it. But it does not need that a high-minded Christian schoolmaster should have been ordained as a priest, in order that he may see the need of such teaching and be able to give it with effect, and in the right spirit.

On the subject of school punishments, Arnold did not profess to be much in advance of his age. All the traditions of the public schools were in favour of flogging. In some of the corporate seals of chartered foundations a rod occupies a conspicuous place as part of the arms or device of an endowed grammar school. For example, the common seal granted to the Louth Grammar School with the letters-patent of Edward the Sixth (1552) represents a pedagogue in the act of inflicting corporal punishment, and contains the legend, *Qui parcit virge odit filium.* The rod was in fact the emblem of discipline, the one characteristic symbol of magisterial authority. Arnold himself said, in one of his letters before going to Rugby: "When I think about this, I long to take rod in hand;"[1] and so far as the younger boys were concerned, he made no apology for retaining the ancient discipline of the public schools. Had he lived in later times, when the theory of education and the study of child nature have received more systematic attention, when other and wiser means of correcting evil have been discovered, and when some of the best-ordered and happy educational communities exist without the employment of physical punishments in any form, he would probably have changed his views on this subject, and acknowledged that in just the proportion in which a skilled teacher understands his business, it becomes less necessary for him to resort to corporal punishment at all. It was with increasing reluctance that he inflicted it, confining it chiefly to moral offences, such as lying, drinking, and habitual idleness, keeping the use of it as much as possible in the background, and for younger scholars only, and regarding it as wholly unsuited as the penalty for intellectual weakness or dulness. Yet to merely sentimental objections to it as degrading to the recipient he would yield nothing. With characteristic directness, he declared that corporal

[1] Letter XXII.

punishment fitly marked and answered to the naturally inferior state of boyhood, and therefore conveyed no peculiar degradation to persons in such a state. "I know well of what feeling this argument about the degrading character of such punishment is the expression. It originates in that proud notion of personal independence, which is neither reasonable nor Christian, but essentially barbarian. It visited Europe with all the curses of the age of chivalry, and is threatening us now with those of Jacobinism. At an age when it is almost impossible to find a true manly sense of the degradation of guilt or faults, where is the wisdom of encouraging a fantastic sense of the degradation of personal correction?" The thought that it was sin which degrades, not the punishment of sin, was ever uppermost in his mind and prominent in his sermons. "What I want to see in the school, and what I cannot find, is an abhorrence of evil. I always think of the psalm, 'Neither doth he abhor anything that is evil.'"

Much of the influence he gained over his scholars — influence which enabled him to dispense in an increasing degree with corporal punishment — was attributable to his knowledge of the individual characteristics of boys. He is said to have known every boy in the school, his appearance, his habits, and his companions. This is a kind of knowledge which has long been known to be characteristic of the disciplinary system of the Jesuits, but has not been common among the head masters of English public schools. Arnold valued it highly and found many opportunities of turning it to useful account. It cannot be said that he was always genial in manner; the younger boys, especially, regarded him with awe, and his own sense of the intense seriousness of life and duty gave a sternness and austerity to his aspect which made many of his pupils afraid of him. He liked to encourage games and sports, though he seldom joined in them, and had a healthy love of bathing, exercise, and long skirmishings in the country. His sympathy with these pursuits showed itself mainly in hasty and occasional visits to the school close. He certainly did nothing to encourage that extravagant passion for athletics, that exaltation of physical prowess to the same level as intellectual distinction, which has in later years so seriously debased the ideal and hindered the usefulness of the great public schools. Mr. Oscar Browning has well said on this point: "The most salient characteristic of modern public schools is the reception of games into the curriculum on an equality with work, if not into a superior position. Of this Arnold would entirely have disapproved. He would have seen that it ministered to a lower standard of effort, that it vulgarized intellectual labour, that it substituted self-indulgence for self-denial, and that it placed those boys in positions of command and influence who were frequently most unfit to exercise either the one or the other."

The danger of the modern "cultus" of sports and athletics is precisely that which Aristotle pointed out in the *Politics* (VIII. 3–35) when he denounced the extreme and violent training which was imposed by the gymnastic exercises of the Spartan youth, as tending to make them "brutal of soul." "Physical courage is not the only end," he urged, "to be aimed at in civil education." A savage and brutal soul is less compatible with exalted courage than a gentle soul trained so as to be exquisitely sensitive to the feelings of shame and honour. The most savage and unfeeling among the barbarian tribes were far from being the most courageous. A man trained on the Lacedemonian system in bodily exercises alone, destitute even of the most indispensable mental culture, was a real βάναυσος, useful only for one branch of political duty, and even for that less useful than if he had been differently trained.[1]

Modern experience in public schools curiously reproduces that of Greece more than two thousand years ago. For the moment the type of school-boy and of manhood most in favour with the British public is Spartan rather than Athenian; but there can be no doubt that Arnold, faithful to the teaching of his own master, would have sought to resist the prevailing fashion, and to confine athletic sports within narrower limits.

The truth is that the Arnoldian tradition which has become slowly evolved and has fixed itself in the minds of most English people, is based more upon Mr. Thomas Hughes' romance, than upon the actual life as set forth in Stanley's volumes. *Tom Brown's School Days* is a manly and spirited book, and is pervaded throughout with a sense of humour, a sym-

[1] See Grote's *Aristotle*, p. 544.

pathy with boyhood, and a love of righteousness and truth. The story is well and vigorously told, and has been deservedly admired. But as Matthew Arnold once said to me, it has been praised quite enough, for it gives only one side, and that not the best side, of Rugby school life, or of Arnold's character. It leaves out of view, almost wholly, the intellectual purpose of a school. It gives the reader the impression that it is the chief business of a public school to produce a healthy animal, to supply him with pleasant companions and faithful friends, to foster in him courage and truthfulness, and for the rest to teach as much as the regulations of the school enforce, but no more. It is to be feared that Hughes' own boyhood was not spent with the best set at Rugby. There were in his time Lake, C. J. Vaughan, Arthur Stanley, Bradley, Lushington, the two Walronds, Matthew and Thomas Arnold, but of these, and of the intense intellectual strain in the sixth form and the upper schoolhouse set, and of the aims by which they were inspired, Hughes appeared to have little or no knowledge. His typical school-boy is seen delighting in wanton mischief, in sport, in a fight, and even in a theft from a farm-yard, distinguished frequently by insolence to inferiors, and even by coarseness and brutality, but not by love of work or by any strong interest in intellectual pursuits. It is after all a one-sided and very imperfect view of ethical discipline, which while it seeks to make a boy sensitive on the point of honour, refusing to "blab" or tell tales of a schoolfellow, is yet tolerant of "cribs" and "vulguses" and other devices by which masters could be hoodwinked or deceived.

This picture of a public school, in spite of its attractive features and of its unquestionable power and reality, will probably be quoted in future years as illustrating the low standard of civilization, the false ideal of manliness, and the deep-seated indifference to learning for its own sake which characterized the upper classes of our youth in the early half of the nineteenth century. In short, the book will be held to explain and justify the famous epithet of "Barbarians" which Matthew Arnold was wont to apply to the English aristocracy and to that section of society which was most nearly influenced by the great public schools.

At the Universities it soon became noticeable, not only that Rugby won an increasing number of academic triumphs, but that the Rugbeians were characterized by a certain gravity and by a deeper seriousness of purpose in life than were to be found among ordinary public-school boys. They were not on that account very popular. The associations which surround ordinary undergraduates, and the talk to which they listen, and the homes from which they come, are not specially calculated to encourage moral thoughtfulness and introspection; and, to say the truth, young people who are prematurely distinguished by these qualities are apt to be regarded as "prigs." Nothing exasperates the average man more than the airs of a superior person, and it may be readily admitted that there was in Arnold's intense earnestness and intellectual aspiration some tendency to beget among his elder pupils self-consciousness and a too pronounced scorn for what satisfies commonplace people. But, after all, this danger, though a real one, is not that from which English society and English boyhood are likely to suffer much. Most of the faults and shortcomings of the British "barbarian" lie in the opposite direction. And an infusion into our social system of a few men with high and even impossible ideals, and with too much earnestness, may well be borne by John Bull without much complaining or loss.

It may be said generally that Arnold's conception of a school was that it should be first of all a place for the formation of character, and next a place for learning and study, as a means for the attainment of this higher end. Discipline and guidance were in his view still more prominently the business of a schoolmaster than the impartation of knowledge. The motives he sought to develop and strengthen were the love of righteousness, the admiration of valour, genius, and patriotism, the sense of duty to others and the scorn of what was little, untruthful, mean, or base in daily action. But the main condition on which the incidental attainment of this object was possible was that the community should be *au fond* pervaded with the spirit of work, and that the proper business of a good school, the production of exact and accomplished scholars, should be thoroughly well fulfilled. Thomas Carlyle, who stayed a week at Rugby, characterized the school as a "temple of industrious peace." This would hardly be an accurate description of a modern public school in which boat races and football matches are the prominent topics of discussion and furnish the chief fields of ambition.

One of the most distinguished of Arnold's successors in the head-mastership of Rugby, Dr. Percival, now the Lord Bishop of Hereford, in writing to me has thus summarized his estimate of Arnold's school work and personal influence:

"If I were called upon to express in a sentence or two my feeling in regard to Dr. Arnold's influence on school life, I should describe him as a great prophet among schoolmasters, rather than an instructor or educator in the ordinary sense of the term. Some are appointed to be prophets, and some pastors and teachers, and he was undoubtedly one of the greatest in the first of these classes. I remember asking Dean Stanley if Arnold taught them a great deal in the sixth form in the course of his lessons, and in reply to my question the Dean held up a little notebook which he happened to have in his hand at the moment, and said, 'I could put everything that Arnold ever taught me in the way of instruction into this little book.'

"Thus it might fairly be said of him, as was said of a famous Oxford leader the other day, that his influence was stimulative rather than formative, the secret of his power consisting not so much in the novelty of his ideas or methods, as in his commanding and magnetic personality, and the intensity and earnestness with which he impressed his views, and made them — as a prophet makes his message — a part of the living forces of the time.

"The dominating idea of his Rugby life was that a head master is called of God to make his school a Christian school, an idea which has no doubt been enthroned in the hearts of multitudes of other schoolmasters, both before and since; but he was destined to make it a new power in the world through the intensity with which he nursed it as a prophetic inspiration, and preached it in all his words and works with a prophetic fervour. This idea pervades not only his chapel sermons, but all the activities of his life. In his lessons, his study of history, his discipline, his exhortations addressed to the sixth form, and to the whole school, and his dealings with individual boys, he is felt to be always striving to infuse into the common life his own enthusiasm of Christian earnestness, and to stimulate the growth of public spirit, moral thoughtfulness, and what we sum up as Christian character.

"Such, I take it, is the best part of the inheritance we owe to him, as it is the food and sustenance of all our highest hopes for the future of English schools."

CHAPTER VI

Arnold's extra-scholastic interests — Why such interests are necessary for a teacher — Foreign travel — Extracts from diary — Love of Nature — Intercourse with the poor needed by himself and by his pupils — University settlements and mission work in connexion with public schools — Politics — The Reform Bill — The Englishman's Register — The society for the diffusion of useful knowledge — Mechanics' Institutes — The London University — Arnold's attitude towards each of these enterprises

It is impossible for readers to understand the true significance of a life or to estimate the value of a man's work without taking into account the pursuits and tastes which have lain outside of his professional duties. It is a familiar truism that we come into the world not only to get a living but to live; and that the life we live depends as much upon the tastes we form, the number and variety of the interests which appeal to us, as upon the manner in which our definite and ostensible work is done. A life wholly devoted to professional duty is necessarily an incomplete life. That duty can only be seen in its true proportions, can, in fact, only be properly discharged at all when its relation to the larger interests which lie outside of it is clearly perceived. This is true of all human employments. But it is especially true in regard to the office of a teacher. There is an inevitable closeness in the intellectual atmosphere of a schoolroom, and the best teachers are precisely those who are most conscious of the need of some sphere of activity beyond its walls. Nothing serves so well to keep the life of a schoolmaster sweet and wholesome as a love for some study or employment which he pursues for its own sake, and which has no immediate and visible relation to the routine of teaching or to the passing of examinations. Pedantry and donnishness, the characteristic faults of the teacher's calling, are wont to be encouraged by the constant exercise of authority in a little world composed entirely of his intellectual inferiors, by the habitual use of the imperative mood, and by an exclusive, albeit conscientious, absorption in scholastic functions. We all need, if we would see our work in true perspective, a vivid sense of the richness and spaciousness of the world outside and some contact with its greater interests, especially those which touch most nearly the borderland of our own profession and home. And we can never understand Arnold's educational work unless we enquire how he employed his leisure, and what were his relations to the larger world of thought and action, of which, after all, a school is only a part.

Arnold was very conscious of the limitations which his profession imposed, and of the danger of sinking to the rank of a mere dominie. And he found the needful expansion in more directions than one. Foreign travel was to him one of the most effective and the most delightful expedients for correcting the tendency to professional narrowness and pedantry. He felt refreshed and invigorated by it.

"I am come out alone, my dearest," he says in one of his home letters, "to see the morning sun on Mont Blanc, and the lake, and to look, I trust, with more than outward eyes on this glorious scene. It is overpowering like all intense beauty, if you dwell on it, but I contrast it immediately with our Rugby horizon and my life of duty there, and our cloudy sky of England, clouded alas! socially, far more than physically. . . . And if, as I trust it will, this rambling and this beauty of nature in foreign lands shall have strengthened me for my work in England, then we may both rejoice that we have had this little parting."

It is noticeable that there is little or no evidence in his letters or journals of any interest in what is generally called "art." There are no raptures about the great painters. He doubtless visited the Uffizi gallery at Florence, the Accademia at Venice, and the galleries of the Vatican, but none of them moved or inspired him much, and he says little or nothing about their treasures. Nor, except once at Pisa, did the architecture of the great Italian cathedrals, the music, the solemn procession, or the mere picturesqueness of the ceremonial of the Roman church, win from him either admiration or criticism. "I care little for the sight of the churches, and nothing at all for the recollection of them. St. John Lateran is the finest of them, and the form of the Greek cross at St. Maria degli Angeli is much better for these buildings than that of the Latin. But precious marbles and gilding and rich colouring are to me like the kaleidoscope and no more, and these churches are almost as inferior to ours, in my judgment, as their worship is to ours."

So it may be said with some truth, that he was deficient in æsthetic sensibility so far as the fine arts were concerned. But he had a keen and loving eye for the beauties of Nature, and his letters are filled with passages showing minute observation of the scenery through which he passed, and testifying also to the delight with which such experience filled his heart. Though his tastes were not materially influenced by poetry, and although imaginative literature generally had little charm for him, he had caught much of the Wordsworthian spirit. It was not merely as a picture that the loveliness of the outward world of hill and valley, of rock and cataract, of gloom and sunshine, appealed most to him. He was, like Wordsworth,

"— well pleased to recognize
In Nature and the language of the sense
The anchor of my purer thoughts, the nurse,
The guide and guardian of my heart, and soul
    Of all my moral being."

And his sense of the richness and glory of the visible world was keenest when he could associate them with the doings and the character of the people who lived on it. It was as an arena for human activity that Europe and its physical characteristics seemed to him best worth studying, and the influence of natural scenery on history, industry, and national welfare filled a larger space in his thoughts than the gratification of æsthetic sensibility. As an example of the accuracy of his observation, this passage from one of his letters may be fitly cited:

"We crossed the Tiber a little beyond Perugia, where it was a most miserable ditch with hardly water enough to turn a mill; indeed, most of the streams which flow from the Apennines were altogether dried up, and the dry and thirsty appearance of everything was truly oriental. The flowers were a great delight to me, and it was very beautiful to see the hedges full of the pomegranate in full flower, the bright scarlet blossom is so exceedingly ornamental, to say nothing of one's associations with the fruit. What we call the Spanish broom of our gardens is the common wild broom of the Apennines, but I do not think it is so beautiful as our own. The fig trees were most luxuriant, but not more so than in the Isle of Wight, and I got tired of the continual occurrence of fruit trees, chiefly olives, instead of large forest trees. The vale of Florence looks quite pale and dull in comparison of our rich valleys, from the total want of timber, and in Florence itself there is not a tree. How miserably inferior to Oxford is Florence altogether, both within, and as seen from a distance; in short, I never was so disappointed in any place in my life. My favourite towns were Genoa, Milan, and Verona. The situation of the latter, just at the foot of the Alps, and almost encircled, like Durham, by a full and rapid river, the Adige, was very delightful."[1]

As an illustration of the alacrity with which he seized on any link between the present and the past, and turned from the observation of the material surroundings and people to the consideration of their history and character, this extract may be quoted from the diary (1828) in which he describes his first view of the Rhine and of Cologne.

"We burst upon the view of the valley of the Rhine, the city of Cologne with all its towers, the Rhine itself distinctly

[1] Letter XVI.

seen at the distance of seven miles, the Seven Mountains above Bonn on our right, and a boundless sweep of the country beyond the Rhine in front of us. To be sure, it was a striking contrast to the first view of the valley of the Tiber from the Mountains of Viterbo; but the Rhine in mighty recollections will vie with anything, and this spot was particularly striking. Cologne was Agrippa's colony inhabited by Germans, brought from beyond the river, to live as the subjects of Rome; the river itself was the frontier of the Empire, — the limit as it were of two worlds, that of Roman laws and customs, and that of German. For before us lay the land of our Saxon and Teutonic forefathers, the land uncorrupted by Roman or any other mixture, the birthplace of the most moral races of men that the world has yet seen, of the soundest laws, the least violent passions, and the fairest domestic and civil virtues. I thought of that memorable defeat of Varus and his three legions, which for ever confined the Romans to the western side of the Rhine, and preserved the Teutonic nation — the regenerating element in modern Europe — safe and free."

But it was not merely to physical exercise and to acquaintance with foreign lands that he turned for the needful refreshment and solace, and for the means of enlarging the sphere of his own interests beyond the walls of the schoolroom. Even when at Laleham, he felt the need of distraction of another kind. Not only enjoyment, but fresh and different duty, seemed to him needful to restore the balance of life, and to save him from the fate of becoming a mere pedagogue. And one of the duties which he found most helpful for this purpose was that of making himself more closely acquainted with the condition and the feelings of the poor. He said in a letter to his friend Tucker:

"I care not a straw for the labour of the half year; for it is not labour but vexation which hurts a man, and I find my comfort depends more and more on the pupils' good and bad conduct. They are an awful charge, but still to me a very interesting one, and one which I could cheerfully pursue till my health or faculties fail me. Moreover, I have now taken up the care of the Workhouse, *i.e.* as far as going there once a week to read prayers and give a sort of lecture upon some part of the Bible. I wanted to see more of the poor people, and I found that unless I devoted a regular time to it I should never do it, for the hunger for exercise, on the part of myself and my horse, used to send me out riding as soon as my work was done. Whereas now I give up Thursday to the village, and it will be my own fault if it does not do me more good than the exercise would." [1]

The belief that the life of a scholar might easily become too isolated and selfish a life, that a knowledge of the needs and feelings of the poor and of the unprivileged classes was a valuable part of education, and that the possession of intellectual advantages carried with it the obligation to do something for those who did not possess them, became stronger as experience brought him more into contact with the sons of rich men and made him more familiar with the peculiar temptations of their life. The memory of the wholesome tonic influence which had become so valuable to himself, when visiting the workhouse at Laleham, remained with him through life. In the course of two remarkable sermons, XXII. and XXIII., on a single episode in our Lord's life, his eating and drinking with a mixed company and in the house of

[1] Letter XII.

Levi the publican, he took occasion to warn young men against the dangers of selfish isolation, either in the scholar's life or in the life of what is called "society,"— the companionship of those of one's own station and of pursuits akin to one's own. Speaking of Christ's example and the kind of intercourse with our fellow-creatures which is calculated to do us most good, he said:

"We dare not in this case trust ourselves in the society of publicans and sinners, we should not do good to them, but they would rather infect us with their own evil. But the natural remedy for our peculiar dangers, the way in which we can best mix with our brethren for the nourishment of our affections, is to be found in the intercourse with our own families on the one hand, and with the poor on the other."

On the former of these points, the necessity of cultivating to the fullest the family affections, he always spoke with peculiar emphasis. Singularly blessed as he was with a happy home, accustomed to do much of his literary work in the room in which wife and children were around him, and deriving strength and inspiration from their presence, the boys could never fail to see how the domestic life was the centre round which all his thoughts clustered. The picture described by a pupil of the fireside at Laleham may remind us of the story of Melanchthon, who was found by the Pope's legate intently studying his Greek Testament held in one hand, while he rocked the cradle with the other. And it is very characteristic of the extent to which he himself was sensitive to the sweet and gracious influences of home, that he took occasion to object even to the apparently innocent and useful institution of reading parties for the long vacation as being not without its drawbacks.

"I cannot but think that a most evil habit has of late years grown up amongst young men when engaged in reading — that of going away from their homes and fixing themselves, for three or four months, in some remote part of the country, where they might study without interruption. It may be that more is thus read than would be read at home, though scarcely more than might be; but even supposing it to be so, it is a dangerous price that is paid for it. The simple quiet of a common family circle, the innumerable occasions of kindness that it affords, and its strong tendency to draw away our thoughts from self and to awaken our affections for others, — a discipline precious at every period of life, — can then least of all be spared when the hardnesses of the world are just coming upon us, when our studies and even our animal spirits are all combining to make us selfish and proud."

On the second point — the need of keeping open the sympathies and of redressing whatever of evil is in the life of the wealthy, by friendly and yet unpatronizing intercourse with the poor — he was wont to be yet more emphatic. At Rugby, as at Laleham, he had put himself, so far as opportunity served, into communication with working men and women, and had derived great benefit from the experience.

"Another way of mixing with our brethren in a manner most especially pleasing to Christ and useful to others, is by holding frequent intercourse with the poor. Perhaps to young men of the richer classes there is nothing which makes their frequent residence in large towns so mischievous to them as the difficulties which they find in the way of such intercourse. In the country, many a young man knows something at least of his poorer neighbours; but in towns, the numbers of the poor, and the absence of any special connexion between him and any of them in particular, hinders him too often from knowing anything of them at all, — an evil which is as much to be regretted on the one side as on the other, and which is quite as mischievous to the minds and tempers of the rich as it is to the bodily condition of the poor. I can hardly imagine anything more useful to a young man of an active and powerful mind, advancing rapidly in knowledge and with high distinction either actually obtained or close in prospect, than to take him — or, much better, that he should go of himself — to the abodes of poverty, of sickness, and old age. Everything there is a lesson; in everything Christ speaks, and the spirit of Christ is ready to convey to his heart all that he witnesses. Accustomed to all the comforts of life, and hardly ever thinking what it would be to want them, he sees poverty in all its evils, — scanty room, and too often scanty fuel, scanty clothing, and scanty food. Instead of the quietness and neatness of his own chamber, he finds very often a noise and a confusion which would render deep thought impossible; instead of the stores of knowledge with which his own study is filled, he finds perhaps only a prayer-book and a Bible. . . . He will see old age and sickness and labour borne not only with patience, but with thankfulness, through the aid of that Bible and the grace of the Holy Spirit who is its author. He will find that while *his* language and studies would be utterly unintelligible to the ears of those whom he is visiting, yet that *they* in their turn have a language and feelings to which he is no less a stranger. . . . It would, indeed, be a blessed thing, and would make this place really a seminary of true religion and useful learning, if those among us who are of more thoughtful years, and especially those of us who are likely to become ministers of Christ hereafter, would remember that their Christian education has commenced already, and that he cannot learn in Christ's school who does not acquaint himself something with the poor. Two or three at first, five or six afterwards, a very small number, might begin a practice, which under proper regulations and guided by Christian prudence, as well as actuated by Christian love, would be equally beneficial to the poor and to yourselves."[1]

We have in these sermons an indication that to learn to be of service to others was a great part of his own education, and that it should also be set forth before the young, as an indispensable part of theirs. The belief that the well-born and the prosperous have as much to learn from intercourse with the poor, as the poor could possibly learn in return, was founded on his own experience and was imparted, as occasion served, to his elder boys. This belief has since his time found expression in many ways. The University Settlements in the South and East of London, Toynbee Hall, the efforts of Eton, Marlborough, and other public schools to maintain different forms of missionary and social enterprise in the poorer suburbs of London, are, though of later date, all in their way legitimate products of Arnold's influence, of the spirit which he sought to infuse into school and University life, the enthusiasm of humanity, the struggle against selfishness and narrowness, and the belief that a good education, like all other privileges, implies a corresponding obligation towards

[1] Sermon XXIII.

those who are without it. By way of further antidote to the narrowing influence of his professional duties, Stanley notices Arnold's Lectures to Mechanics' Institutes at Rugby and Lutterworth, his frequent sermons to village congregations, the establishment of a dispensary, his tracts of advice on the appearance of the cholera; and, at the time of the construction of the railway, his exertions to procure the sanction of the Bishop to the performance of short services for the labourers employed on it, to be conducted by himself and his assistant masters in turn.

There were circumstances in the political and social life of the kingdom at the time which were well calculated to occasion grave anxiety, and to stimulate an ardent reformer like Arnold with a desire to take a part in public life. The period of the Reform Bill happened to coincide with the prevalence of much distress and industrial unrest. The resolute resistance of the Duke of Wellington and the Tory party to the enactment of that measure embittered the temper of the unenfranchised classes; and the increasing use of steam mechanism, both for manufactures and for locomotion, caused a dislocation in our industrial system, closed up some of the avenues to employment, and excited considerable alarm among the working classes. Arnold took the keenest interest in the angry and, as it seemed to him, somewhat perilous conflicts of the time. He believed that the social dangers which threatened the nation could only be averted by the exercise of more sympathy on the part of the ruling classes, and more intelligence on the part of the ruled. So he determined to venture on a new periodical, the *Englishman's Register*, which lived a brief life, from May to July, 1831.

"I want," he said, "to get up a real Poor Man's Magazine, which should not bolster up abuses and veil iniquities, nor prose to the poor as to children, but should address them in the style of Cobbett, plainly, boldly, and in sincerity, excusing nothing, concealing nothing, and misrepresenting nothing, but speaking the very whole truth in love."[1]

It is very characteristic of him that he plunged into this chivalrous enterprise before he had well assured himself of probable support from friends and sympathizers, and before he had adequately estimated the serious pecuniary obligations which it entailed.

"Our hope is," he said, in his introductory article, "to rally those, and we believe there are many who feel in these tremendous times as we do, who are disgusted alike with the folly and iniquity that would keep all things as they are, and with the no less foolish and unprincipled violence which would destroy rather than reform, and which pollutes even reform itself by its unchristian spirit and resentments."

Accordingly, he contributed to the paper some vigorous articles in favour of the reform of the representative system, and interspersed them with other articles on the labouring classes, and with a series of expository articles on the book of Genesis, and on the lessons which might be derived from it in relation to the right economy and use of life. After the discontinuance of the *Register* he contributed to the

[1] Letter XXVI.

Sheffield Courant a succession of letters on the social condition of the operative classes, which dealt with such topics as labour, wages, poverty, education, and reform in a manner which is no less remarkable for the sympathy with which he viewed the condition, the needs, and the aspirations of the poor, than for the earnestness with which he warned them against indulging in illusions. He told the working classes frankly that they must not expect too much from parliamentary reform, and he refuted the doctrine that war was good because it furnished employment and made trade brisk. He would not have working men suppose that any nostrum or political arrangement could ever save them from the responsibility of qualifying themselves by their own industry and intelligence for a larger share of the comfort and social advantages of life. Some of his articles in the defunct *Register* and in the *Sheffield Courant* were republished by Stanley in a supplementary volume of Miscellaneous Works. They may still be read with interest by any one who desires to study the economic history as well as the temper of the times. For example, he dwelt on the natural tendency of wealth to become richer and poverty poorer. The effect of wealth, he said, was to make men more alive to intellectual pleasures and more able to procure them, while poverty renders the same pleasures at once undesired and unattainable. In this way the two classes of our community have been removed from one another by a greater distance, and have become strangers, if not enemies. The excess of aristocracy in our whole system—religious, political, and social—had led to an enormous evil, though it was hard to say that any one was to blame for it. The rich and poor have each a distinct language, the language of the rich being that of books, and being full of French words derived from Roman ancestors, while that of the poor retained its Anglo-Saxon character.

"Our business," he said, "is to raise all and lower none. Equality is the dream of a madman, or the passion of a fiend. Extreme inequality, or high comfort and civilization in some, coexisting with deep misery and degradation in others, is no less also a folly and a sin. But an equality in which some have all the enjoyments of civilized life, and none are without its comforts, where some have all the treasures of knowledge, and none are sunk in ignorance,—that is a social system in harmony with the order of God's creation in the natural world."[1]

There were other public movements which were not political and were of a more hopeful kind. Lord Brougham, whose reforming zeal made him many enemies, and whose restless and versatile energy alienated many who were disposed to sympathize with his measures, had, as early as 1816, distinguished himself in Parliament by setting on foot the first enquiry into the "abuses of the public charitable foundations connected with education," and had also initiated another enquiry into the state of education in the metropolis. Failing, after repeated efforts, to arouse Parliament to any strong interest in the sub-

[1] *Sheffield Courant*, 1832. Letter II.

ject, he, in 1825, allied himself with Romilly, Lord John Russell, W. Tooke, James Mill, Henry Hallam, M. D. Hill, Sir Charles Bell, Bishop Maltby of Durham, William Allen, and other prominent Whigs, in the establishment of a voluntary Society for the Diffusion of Useful Knowledge. In 1828 the society was able to congratulate its supporters on the success "which had attended its efforts to make the most useful and the most exalted truths of science easily and generally accessible." In that year Charles Knight became the recognized publisher, and up to the year 1846, when the society came to an end, a succession of treatises and tracts appeared which undoubtedly had a most stimulating effect on the intellectual life of the working classes, and especially on the class immediately above them. Very eminent writers were engaged. Brougham himself contributed the opening treatise on the "objects, advantages, and pleasures of science." Dr. Lardner, Sir James Mackintosh, Professor Malden, were among the other contributors. The *Library of Useful Knowledge*, the *Penny Cyclopædia*, which appeared at first in penny weekly numbers, the *Library of Entertaining Knowledge*, and the *Penny Magazine*, which was the pioneer of many periodicals of mingled instruction and entertainment, were all new experiments in popular literature, and were welcomed by many good men as enterprises of high value and far-reaching influence.

A kindred effort, mainly helped forward by the same persons, was the establishment by Dr. Birkbeck, in 1820, of the first Mechanics' Institution in London.

The example was widely followed in the provincial towns. Classes, reading rooms, and libraries were provided, courses of lectures on science were arranged, and great efforts were made to popularize knowledge and to attract working men to the Institutes. Under different names — Literary Institutes, Polytechnics, Evening Continuation Classes — the Mechanics' Institute survives in full and beneficial activity to our own day; but it should not be forgotten that the first serious attempt in England to provide in the evening for those who had been laboriously engaged during the day, means and appliances for intellectual culture was made by Brougham, Birkbeck, and the promoters of the "Diffusion Society."

A still more ambitious enterprise was the foundation, in 1828, of an institution intended to serve as a University for London. At that time religious tests were enforced at the older Universities practically excluding from the benefits of those foundations all who felt unable or unwilling to sign the thirty-nine articles. The expense of living at Oxford or Cambridge placed their advantages out of the reach of many poor students; and before the creation of railways, even the distance of these centres of learning from the metropolis was felt to be a disadvantage. In these circumstances Thomas Campbell, the poet, had published, in 1825, a letter addressed to Lord Brougham, earnestly advocating the establishment in London of a great University for "teaching, examining, exercising, and rewarding with honours in the liberal arts and sciences the youth of our middling rich people," — a University combining the advantages of public and private education, the emulative spirit produced "by examination before numbers, and by honours conferred before the public, the cheapness of domestic residence, and all the moral influences that result from home." Shares representing £160,000 were taken up, and in 1827 the foundation of the new building in Gower Street was laid by the king's brother, the Duke of Sussex. For a time that institution, though it failed to obtain power from the Crown to confer degrees, was known as the London University, and it was not until 1836, after King's College had been founded, that the long negotiations with the Government were terminated by an arrangement which conferred upon each of those Colleges a charter recognizing it as a teaching body; and at the same time incorporated by Charter a third body, to be called the "University of London," with power to examine candidates from those and other affiliated colleges, and to confer academic degrees in any branch of learning or science except theology.

In all these enterprises Arnold had the keenest interest. They seemed to him to be full of promise for the intellectual emancipation and improvement of the whole English people, and he threw himself into them with characteristic vehemence and enthusiasm. He was in full sympathy with the objects which the promoters of the Diffusion Society, the Mechanics' Institutes, and the London University had in view, but he was not without grave misgivings about the methods they adopted. He could not withhold sympathy from the educational reformers, although what Sir G. Trevelyan has somewhat happily called Brougham's "slovenly omniscience" caused that sympathy to be imperfect. The arid and limited conception of "Useful Knowledge," knowledge sought because of its visible relation to practical uses, could not be expected to satisfy him. The publications of the "Diffusion" Society dealt mainly with scientific facts and interesting information, and left almost wholly out of view the culture of the imagination and the taste. There was a singular absence from the Society's programme of the humaner studies, literature, art, logic, ethics, poetry, and philosophy. But these defects, though serious, were in his view not the worst. There was, he thought, an indifference to religion characterizing the publications of the Society, and this chilled and disheartened him most. It was one of his deepest convictions, that while the education of an Englishman need not be sectarian, it should be essentially Christian. "The slightest touch of Christian principle and Christian hope, in the Society's biographical and historical articles," he said in one of his letters, "would be a sort of living salt to the whole." And in another letter he described the sort of literature which he should like to furnish to the working men of England as "Cobbett-like in style, but Christian in spirit." "I never wanted articles on religious subjects half so much as articles on common subjects written with a decidedly Christian tone." And his enthusiasm in favour of directing these new and promising agencies for mental improvement into a course which should recognize the moral and spiritual needs of the nation, took a very practical shape when, in writing to one of the officers of the Diffusion Society, he said:

"I am convinced that if the *Penny Magazine* were decidedly and avowedly Christian, many of the clergy throughout the kingdom would be most delighted to assist its circulation by every means in their power. For myself, I should think that I could not do too much to contribute to the support of what would then be so great a national blessing, and I should beg to be allowed to offer fifty pounds annually towards it so long as my remaining in my present situation enabled me to gratify my inclinations to that extent."

The offer was not accepted. It is difficult, indeed, to conceive how an arrangement, such as Arnold desired, could be formulated and rendered permanent without raising in the Society many formidable theological difficulties. To Arnold himself, who saw his way clearly to the preparation of articles which would fulfil his own ideal, the difficulties seemed to be trifling. The Committee of the Society, however, formed a truer estimate of the public interpretation which would be put on his plan, and determined to adhere resolutely to the course they had from the first adopted. They resolved to make intellectual improvement and useful knowledge their main business, leaving to other agencies all discussions on disputable theology and on morals and religion. Their activity in publication did not slacken, but they worked under limitations which, even to Arnold, appeared to be harmful, and which caused a large

K

number of the ministers of religion to regard the Society with scant sympathy and some suspicion to the last. The *Saturday Magazine*, which was published by the Society for promoting Christian Knowledge, was considered by many as the rival, and by others as the antidote to the *Penny Magazine*, and secured a large circulation. Arnold said to a member of that Society·

"I have had some correspondence with the Useful Knowledge people about their *Penny Magazine*, and have sent them some things which I am waiting to see if they will publish; but of course what I have been doing, and may do, for them does not hinder me from doing what I can for you. I only suspect that I should want to liberalize your magazine, as I wish to Christianize theirs, and probably your Committee would recalcitrate against any such operation, as theirs may do. The Christian Knowledge Society has a bad name for the dulness of its publications, and their contributions to the cause of general knowledge, and enlightening the people in earnest, may seem a little tardy and reluctant."[1]

The Useful Knowledge Society came to an end in 1846. It was an honourable and undoubtedly successful effort to promote the better education of the people, and the influence of its publications long survived its own death. If its promoters proved to be too sanguine, if later experience showed that they made an inaccurate estimate both of the appetite of the working man for intellectual nutriment and of the character of the nutriment to be provided, the partial failure of the enterprise is nowise to their dis-

[1] Letter XLIV.

credit. At least it blocked up one of the roads to future failure, and did much to make later educational progress possible. But Arnold's interest in the larger work of Dr. Birkbeck was not diminished by this partial failure. His lecture on the divisions and mutual relation of knowledge, delivered before the Mechanics' Institute at Rugby, shows at the same time his sympathy with the promoters of such institutions and his desire to improve the ideal of "useful knowledge" which was to a large extent presented to the working classes in the lectures to which they were accustomed. He expressed an earnest wish to encourage Mechanics' Institutes on account of the good that they can do, and at the same time he deemed it important to call attention to their necessary imperfections and to notice the good which they cannot do. There is in this lecture little or no reference to the merely material or commercial value of knowledge, but an attempt to enlarge his hearers' conception of the worth of mental cultivation as a means of enriching life and adding to its power and usefulness. Hence he dwells much on the need of such studies as philosophy, languages, and logic, as helping to foster a love of truth, and to qualify the student to think more soundly and accurately about any of the subjects in which he might become interested, especially those which concerned most nearly the duties of the citizen and the formation of right opinions about the past and the future.

In 1836, he was invited to a seat on the Senate of the newly constituted University of London, and he accepted the post with much alacrity, believing that here was a new opportunity for usefulness and a promising instrument for extending the blessings of a liberal education to many persons who had hitherto been excluded from academic privileges. One of the first proposals which he submitted to the Senate was to the effect that an acquaintance with some part of the New Testament in the original should be required of every candidate for a degree in Arts. For degrees in Law and Medicine he was not disposed to insist on this condition. But a degree in Arts, he contended, ought to certify that the holder had received a complete and liberal education; and a liberal education without the Scriptures must, in any Christian country, be a contradiction in terms. Of theoretic difficulties in the conduct of the examination he made very light.

"I am perfectly ready," he said, "to examine to-morrow in any Unitarian School in England, in presence of parents and masters. I will not put a question that shall offend, yet I will give such an examination as will bring out, or prove the absence of, Christian knowledge of the highest value. I speak as one who has been used to examine young men in the Scriptures for nearly twenty years, and I pledge myself to the perfect easiness of doing this. Our examinations, in fact, will carry their own security with them if our characters will not, and we should not and could not venture to proselytize even if we wished it. But this very circumstance of our having joined the London University at the risk of much odium from a large part of our profession would be a warrant for our entering into the spirit of the Charter with perfect sincerity."[1]

[1] Letter to Bishop Otter, CLXIII.

These views, however, were not accepted by his colleagues on the Senate, many of whom saw with greater clearness than he how difficult it would be to secure a succession of Arnolds as Scripture examiners, and how many promising and conscientious students might possibly be excluded from the University, if the religious examination were insisted on.

Accordingly, his proposal that every candidate for the degree of B.A. should be required to take up one of the Gospels or Epistles at his discretion was rejected. But in deference to his judgment and that of the minority who sympathized with him, a voluntary or supplementary examination was instituted in the Hebrew Text of the Old Testament, the Greek Text of the New Testament, and Scripture History and Evidences, and special prizes and certificates were offered to successful candidates. The regulations for this examination are still in force in the scheme of the London University and are an interesting survival testifying to Arnold's influence. But the annual number of candidates is small, and the certificates in this department of knowledge do not count in any way towards the attainment of a degree. Though keenly regretting that the principle for which he had contended did not obtain the approval of the Senate, Arnold yet continued for a time to serve as a member of that body, partly because he did not wish to censure even by implication those Bishops and clergy who still felt it their duty to remain, and partly in the hope of making the Scriptural examination as attractive and effective as possible, and perhaps of so regulating its conditions that the Arts degree would be generally understood to be incomplete without it. When it afterwards became evident that neither the authorities of the affiliated Colleges, nor those of the University itself, shared his belief in the necessity of such an examination, or were disposed to regard it in any other light than as a purely voluntary exercise, he abandoned the contest, and in a sorrowful and dignified letter addressed to the Chancellor at the end of 1838, he finally resigned all connexion with the University.

CHAPTER VII

The Oxford movement — The Hampden controversy — Arnold's relation to the movement — His views as to the condition of the Church of England and of necessary reforms — Dean Church's estimate of Arnold's ecclesiastical position — The Broad Church — Influence of outside interests on the life of the schoolmaster — The ideal teacher — Regius Professorship of Modern History — Arnold's scheme of lectures — Its partial fulfilment — His early death — Conjectures as to what might have been had he lived — Mr. Forster and the Education Act — Testimonies of Dean Boyle and of the *Times*

IT will easily be gathered from the foregoing pages that Arnold was likely to feel profoundly interested in the remarkable religious revival, which under the name of the Oxford movement made the fourth decade of this century so memorable in the history of the English Church. Indeed, any estimate of his character and career would be incomplete which did not include some reference to his share in that movement. Some of his old associates of the Oriel set, including Keble, Hurrell, Froude, Pusey, Rose, Newman, and others, were led by the study of Church History and by a profound distrust of the current theology of the day, to assume a new position and to be recognized as *par excellence* the Anglican party in the English church. In 1827 Keble published his *Christian Year*, a volume of which Pusey afterwards said, that "it was the unknown dawn and harbinger of the reawakening of deeper truth." In 1833, Newman began the publication of Tracts for the *Times*, with the avowed object of withstanding the liberalism of the day, and of finding a basis for the English church in Catholic antiquity, and strengthening the sacerdotal and sacramental elements in her teaching.[1] In 1835, Pusey started the Library of the Fathers. The series of Tracts came to an end in 1841 with the publication of Tract 90, which was a laboured argument to prove that the articles of the Church of England admitted of a Catholic interpretation. This tract was censured by Bishops and by the Heads of Houses at Oxford, and was received with such a storm of indignation that the publication of the Tracts proceeded no further. The subsequent submission of Newman to the Roman Catholic Church in 1845 was the catastrophe of the movement.

The story of this movement has been told with singular candour, clearness, and dignity, and with touching pathos by John Henry Newman, the protagonist of the drama, in his *Apologia pro vitâ suâ;* and from another point of view, with no less fairness and scarcely less literary charm, in Dean Church's *Oxford Movement*. It must suffice here to refer to such of the incidents of that eventful time as specially interested Arnold and called forth his combative instincts. Dr. R. D. Hampden, who was public examiner in Oxford in 1831–1832, became Bampton lecturer in the following year, and in that capacity preached a course of lectures on the "Scholastic Philosophy considered in its relations to Christian

[1] *Apologia*, pp. 150 and 195.

Theology." It was a scholarly though not very inspiring book; it traced the influence of the Alexandrine divines and of the schoolmen on the formation of the Christian Creeds, and would in our days have been regarded as a thoughtful and useful contribution to Church History, without startling any one by its originality or daring speculation. But by the High Church and Tory party in Oxford the book was then regarded as dangerously latitudinarian in its opinions, chiefly because it exhibited with remorseless frankness the very human elements which entered into the composition of ancient formularies, such as the Nicene and Athanasian Creeds, and so might tend to deprive them of that divine authority which high Anglicans were wont to claim for them. The book was solemnly condemned by the Heads of Houses as unorthodox and dangerous, and when Lord Melbourne, in 1836, proposed to appoint Hampden to the Regius Professorship of Divinity, a strong and acrimonious opposition to the appointment arose in Oxford. The Prime Minister, however, persisted in the nomination, and the only practical effect of the agitation was by a vote in Convocation to exclude the Regius Professor from his place at a Board whose duty it was to nominate University preachers.[1]

---

[1] It was not till after Arnold's death that the same controversy was revived in an aggravated form by the nomination in 1847, of Hampden to the bishopric of Hereford — a nomination which Lord John Russell, the minister of the day, persisted in, notwithstanding remonstrances from the clergy, from the Dean of Hereford, and from thirteen of the bishops.

It was not to be expected that Arnold could keep silent in the midst of this ecclesiastical ferment. He was "ever a fighter," and in regard to questions which touched the interests of religion a strong and even vehement controversialist. He threw himself with characteristic courage and energy into the thickest of the fray. Of what has been cynically called the "nasty little virtue of prudence," it must be owned he was not endowed with a large share. He wrote, in 1829, a pamphlet strongly urging the wisdom and expediency of conceding the Catholic claims. He stayed not to consider whether the outspoken utterance of unpopular opinion would injure his reputation with the governors of the school; and as we have already shown, he refused with courtesy, but with firmness, a request from one of the Rugby trustees that he would declare whether he was or was not the author of an anonymous article in a Review. Freedom to speak his mind on burning questions was a necessity of his being, and he would readily have resigned his mastership, had it been necessary, rather than surrender this freedom. That a cause was for the moment unpopular, was with him almost a *primâ facie* reason for espousing it,

Victrix causa diis placuit, sed victa Catoni.

His famous article in the *Edinburgh Review*, entitled the "Oxford Malignants,"[1] is an example of his

[1] These were the five members of a small committee which met in the common room at Corpus to draw up a protest against Hampden's appointment as Regius Professor, on the ground that "he had contradicted the doctrinal truths which he was pledged to maintain." Eighty-one members of the University signed this protest.

polemical style when specially roused to indignation; and his knowledge of history caused him to feel how impotent was the attempt to prevent the spread of opinions, whether really or only apparently heterodox, by means of ecclesiastical censures.

"He wielded a pen," said J. B. Mozley, "as if it were a ferule." The violent proceedings of the Newmanite party against Hampden were, in his opinion, glaringly unjust. He saw in the *privilegium* voted by Convocation nothing but Lynch law. He saw in it a reproduction in spirit and in essence of the nonjurors reviling Burnet, of the Council of Constance condemning Huss, of the Judaizers banded together against Paul.[1]

As one reads the story of those days, he is reminded of the terms in which Matthew Arnold, many years afterwards, apostrophized Oxford as the "home of lost causes and forsaken beliefs, and unpopular names, and impossible loyalties."[2] Father and son were alike in loving Oxford dearly, and were conscious of their deep and lifelong debt to it. But to both, the influence of the High Church party appeared profoundly mischievous to the true interests of religion and to the welfare and full development of the Church's usefulness. Indeed, Arnold almost despaired of the Church of England, although he believed that it ought to become the main instrument for the moral culture of the nation and for the exaltation of righteousness and truth. The decorous and apologetic

---
[1] *Edinburgh Review*, January, 1845.
[2] Preface to M. Arnold's *Essays in Criticism*.

orthodoxy of the eighteenth century, the negligence and apathy of many of the clergy, and their isolation from the main current of popular interests, repelled and profoundly saddened him. "Our Church," he said, "bears, and has ever borne, the marks of her birth. The child of royal and aristocratic selfishness and unprincipled tyranny, she has never dared to speak boldly to the great, but has contented herself with lecturing the poor. 'I will speak of thy testimonies even before kings, and will not be ashamed,' is a text of which the Anglican Church as a national institution has never caught the spirit." The fact that twenty-two out of twenty-four bishops voted in the House of Lords against the Reform Bill was well calculated to arouse the *sæva indignatio* which, when occasion arose, was so easily excited in him. Here was no case in which the religious interests of the people needed to be safeguarded by the spiritual peers. But the incident brought into strong relief the fatal tendency of English ecclesiastics to identify themselves with the interests of the privileged classes, and seemed to Arnold to render the outlook for the future more dispiriting than ever.

In these circumstances, the new signs of life and energy which the leaders of the Oxford movement were beginning to put forth, and the desire of that party to emancipate itself from political trammels, might have been expected to win Arnold's sympathy. But in his view the whole of that movement was vitiated by the sacerdotal pretensions and claims of some of the clergy, by their revival of some mediæval and outworn superstitions, and by their habit of regarding the acceptance of dogmas as the only basis of Christianity. He had learned from Coleridge a larger conception of the scope and office of a Christian church, whose members should include many of those now called dissenters, and whose ministers should form a *clerisy* — not exclusively teachers of theology, but leaders and helpers in all that concerned the intellectual interests and the social life of the people, in wise philanthropy, and in practical religion.[1] Dean Church thus defines what he conceives to have been Arnold's position at the time:

"Dr. Arnold's view of the Church was very simple. He divided the world into Christians and non-Christians. Christians were all who professed to believe in Christ as a divine person, and to worship him; and the brotherhood — the 'Societas' of Christians — was all that was meant by the Church in the New Testament. It mattered of course to the conscience of each Christian what he had made up his mind to believe, but to no one else. Church organization was according to circumstances partly inevitable or expedient, partly mischievous, but in no case of divine authority. Teaching, ministering the word, was a thing of divine appointment, but not so the mode of exercising it, either as to persons, forms, or methods. Sacraments there were, signs and pledges of divine love and help in every action of life, in every sight of nature, and eminently two most touching ones recommended to Christians by the Redeemer himself; but except as a matter of mere order, one man might deal with them as lawfully as another."[2]

[1] Coleridge's *Church and State.*
[2] Dean Church, *The Oxford Movement,* p. 6.

He advocated the abolition of tests in the Universities, the opening of the church's doors to the admission of dissenters, the abandonment of the practice of translating Bishops from one diocese to another, the equalization of incomes, the formation of new parishes, and the revival of the order of deacons. But his utterances on these subjects were not acceptable to any party in the English church, and it pained and distressed him to find how many enemies he made. One of those parties appeared to him narrow, timid, and at the same time fanatical in their Bibliolatry and their demands for evangelical orthodoxy, and another to be putting forth personal claims to priestly authority which he regarded as wholly alien to the spirit of Christianity. At any rate, he received little sympathy from either. "If I had two necks," he said, "I should have a good chance of being hanged by both sides." His unpopularity was shown by the refusal of the Archbishop of Canterbury to allow him to preach the sermon at Lambeth on the consecration of Stanley, the Bishop of Norwich. His attitude towards the reforming party in the Church on the one hand, and to the older orthodoxy on the other, reminds one of that of Erasmus, who though sympathizing with Luther in his denunciation of negligence, corruption, and superstition, was unwilling to weaken the Church or to deny her primitive teaching. "Instead of leading," Erasmus sadly complains, "I have stood naked and unarmed between the javelins of two angry foes."

It would appear that he had formed an ideal of a

Christian state organized on some such model as his own school at Rugby, with a chief magistrate, energetic, God-fearing, and wise, with the clergy and aristocracy a sort of sixth form, exercising large influence in the repression of evil and encouragement of good, and a whole community not necessarily holding one set of opinions, but willing to share the same worship and to work together as the servants of the same Divine Master. Neither in a State nor in his school was he disposed to regard uniformity as the test of excellence. In his opinion intellectual freedom, and diversity in creed and organization were wholly compatible with unity of Christian purpose and with corporate national life.

It would be foreign to my present purpose to enter further into details respecting Arnold's religious life, and his strivings against what seemed to him the worldliness of the Church and in favour of wider Christian comprehension. "The identity of the Christian commonwealth with the Christian state was the vision that had inspired the ecclesiastical polity of Hooker. It was the ruling thought of Selden's grave sense, of Burke's high political philosophy, and of the religious philosophy of Coleridge."[1] To this may be added that it had been the dream of Chillingworth, and has been, in different forms, that of Arthur Stanley, of Frederick Maurice, of Whateley, of Bunsen and of Jowett, of Phillips Brooks, the late Bishop of Massachusetts, and of many another large-souled man who sought to make

[1] *Life of Dean Stanley*, Vol. II., p. 176.

Christian men lay aside minor differences and agree to combine together in religious sympathy, in the advancement of righteousness, and in strenuous Christian work. But it is a dream which has never been realized, and, so far as we can see, after more than half a century, is not likely to be realized. Arnold believed that so long as the only unity the churches can understand means uniformity of belief and opinion, and not identity in moral and spiritual aim; so long as the battle of the sects is a fight for creeds rather than a war against sin and ignorance, unity is simply impossible in any country in which there is any intellectual life at all. While each section of the Christian community attaches more importance to the dogmas and usages by which that section is distinguished from the rest, than to the fundamental aims in which they are all practically agreed, every effort to secure greater comprehensiveness in the Church and unity in Christendom seems foredoomed to failure. And those who shared his views must have sorrowfully admitted that in this matter Arnold was only beating the air, and that the problem he mused over and vehemently discussed is, for the present at least, insoluble. Yet something will survive, — something always does survive from honest striving after a generous and noble, even if an unattainable, ideal. When much that is ephemeral in theological controversy is forgotten, the aspirations of those who have sought to discover a deeper foundation for spiritual unity than that of ecclesiastical creeds and systems will abide as permanent factors in the history of religion. To men with such aspirations it is a relief to turn from the polemics of rival schools, from the Oxford movement, from Tract Ninety, from discussions about the Hampden controversy or the Eastward position, to the calm and gracious utterances of one who said: "Other sheep I have which are not of this fold. Them also must I bring, and they shall hear my voice and there shall be one flock and one Shepherd."

No apology is needed, even in a book mainly addressed to teachers, for dwelling with so much detail on the extra-scholastic aspects of Arnold's life. For indeed, the influence of a schoolmaster is largely conditioned by the pursuits and tastes which characterize him out of school, and by the nature of his outlook into the life on which his pupils are about to embark. His love of foreign travel served to illuminate his lessons, to increase his descriptive power, and to help boys better to know something of the world, and of their own place in it. His historical imagination enabled him to arouse their sympathies for the great men of old and their aspirations after the nobler kinds of fame and success. His insatiable thirst for knowledge kept his mind fresh and receptive, made the life of the scholar more attractive in the eyes of the boys, and prevented him from losing touch with young learners, to whom all knowledge was new. His militant political liberalism, though not obtruded in school, could not fail to leaven a community largely composed of the sons of rich men, and it unconsciously helped them to become aware of their duties to the unprivileged classes, especially to the poor and the ignorant. His domestic life, in a singularly happy and tranquil home, kept his affections pure and tender, and caused him to bring the intuitions of a parent to rectify his merely professional knowledge of boys and their capacities, their needs, and their dangers. Above all, the profound religiousness of his nature and his solemn sense of duty coloured the whole of his acts and thoughts, and gave to all those who came most under his influence an almost premature sense of the seriousness of life and of the responsibilities of Christian manhood.

Thus his life reveals to us the manifold and varied nature of the equipment of a true teacher. Scholarship alone is but a part, and not necessarily the highest part, of that equipment. Strong will and force of character are great and indeed indispensable endowments for a head master. Physical activity and abounding hopefulness are not less needed. All these Arnold possessed. "I suppose," he once said, "the desirable feeling to entertain is always to expect to succeed, and never to think you have succeeded." But more is necessary to make the ideal teacher. He needs an insight into child nature and into the processes by which truth can be communicated, faith in the boundless possibilities of good which lie even in the most unpromising and uninteresting scholars, a deep sympathy with every form of youthful weakness except sin, and a genuine enthusiasm and love for work. The best teacher in the world must always fall short in some respects of this ideal; but it was because Arnold ever kept it in view, and strove with all his might to realize it, that his name will long remain in our history as that of a great schoolmaster, who ennobled his profession, and fulfilled, though in a way hardly anticipated by Hawkins, the remarkable prophecy that he would transform the public schools of England.

One of the most gratifying incidents of his life was his appointment, in 1842, to the Regius Professorship of Modern History at Oxford. The compliment thus paid to him was peculiarly welcome. It was an honourable recognition of his eminent industry and success in his favourite field of research; it renewed his connexion with his beloved Oxford; it brought around him once more many of his former friends; and it served to soften, if not to obliterate, the memories of some personal controversies. A contemporary letter of R. W. Church, afterwards Dean of St. Paul's, who was living at Oriel, in February, 1842, describes vividly the impression left upon a young and not wholly sympathetic College don of that period.

"The great lion at present is Arnold and his lectures which have created a great stir in the exalted, the literary, and the fashionable world of Oxford. He is here with his whole family, and people look forward to his lectures in the theatre day after day, as they might to a play. He will be quite missed when he goes. Almost every Head goes with his wife and daughters, if he has any, and so powerful is Arnold's eloquence, that the Master of Balliol was, on one occasion, quite overcome, and fairly went — not quite into hysterics, but into tears — upon which the Provost remarked at a large party, that he supposed it was the gout."

"However, they are very striking lectures. He is working out his inaugural. Everything he does, he does with life and force, and I cannot help liking his manly and open way, and the great reality which he throws about such things as description of country, military laws and operations, and such like low concerns. He has exercised on the whole a generous forbearance towards us and let us off with a few angular points about Priesthood and the Puritans in one lecture, while he has been immensely liberal in other ways, and I should think not to the taste of the Capitular body, *e.g.* puffing with all his might the magnificent age and intensely interesting contests of Innocent III, and in allowing any one to believe, without any suspicion of superstition, a very great many of Bede's miracles and some others besides."[1]

The lectures on Modern History, fragmentary and incomplete as they are, serve well to illustrate the character of Arnold's mind. He was, as it has been said, an "insatiable reader, an active controversialist, in whose view every series of phenomena naturally crystallized into a theory." The province of history, the characteristics of historical style, military ethics, military geography, national prejudices, religious and political parties in England, are among the topics rather glanced at than discussed in these lectures.[2] His first intention was to begin with the year 1400, in the hope of doing for England a similar service to that which Guizot had then undertaken to

[1] Dean Church's *Life and Letters*, p. 35.
[2] *Edinburgh Review*, January, 1843.

do for France. He meant to trace the change of property produced by the Wars of the Roses, and the growth of the English aristocracy, as it gradually superseded in power the aristocracy of purely Norman descent. He afterwards abandoned the plan and began at an earlier date. The statutes required that terminal lectures on biography should be given in connexion with the historical courses, and this was a requirement peculiarly congenial to Arnold, and in conformity with his own method of instruction. He had always held that the way to vivify history and make it impressive and useful was to connect it with the lives and characters of typical men. So he planned a series of discourses on Gregory the Great, Charlemagne, Alfred, Dante, and other representative men of the pre-Reformation period. But these visions were never realized. The first course of professorial lectures proved to be his last.

The end came suddenly. On the morning of Sunday, the 12th of June, 1842, the day before his forty-seventh birthday, he succumbed to a sharp attack of *angina pectoris*, the disease from which his father had died. Of the shock and bewilderment which this event caused in his household, and throughout the little community of Rugby, Dean Stanley's pages contain a touching description, which could not properly be simplified or shortened or reproduced here. Of those whom he left behind him, Jane, the eldest daughter, became the wife of William Edward Forster, afterwards M.P. for Bradford and Vice-President of the Committee of Council on

Education; Matthew was the eldest son; Thomas, the second son, became a Fellow of his college at Oxford, and has devoted himself to literary and educational work; William Delafield Arnold was for a time director of public instruction in the Punjaub, and died on his way homewards in 1859; and Edward was a clergyman and inspector of schools. In the next generation, Mrs. Humphry Ward, the gifted daughter of Thomas, and the author of *Robert Elsmere*, and Mr. H. O. Arnold Forster, M.P. for Belfast, the son of W. D. Arnold, have in different ways achieved honourable reputation.

Speculation in reference to what Arnold's future career might have been were obviously fruitless. Not improbably he would have become a liberal Bishop, and it may be conjectured that in that capacity he might have grown more tolerant of extreme opinions and have found out the use which the Church may make of extreme men. But it is hardly to be believed that he would have ever been reconciled to the developments of modern ritualism. Still less was he likely to be satisfied with the sacerdotal claims of the clergy, or with the belief that the Anglicanism of the thirty-nine articles represented the final stage in the development of the Christian church. There is a remarkable passage in a letter of Matthew Arnold to his mother in 1862, in which, speaking of the Colenso controversy and the timid and apologetic character of the orthodox defence, he says:

"I do not think it possible for a clergyman to treat these matters satisfactorily. In Papa's time it was so, but it is so, it seems to me, no longer. He is the last free speaker of the Church of England, who speaks without being shackled, and without being aware that he is so and that he is in a false position in consequence: the moment a writer feels this his power is gone. I may add that if a clergyman does not feel this now he ought to feel it. The best of them, Jowett for example, obviously do feel it. I am quite sure Papa would have felt it had he been living now and thirty years younger. Not that he would have been less a Christian, or less zealous for a National Church, but his attention would have been painfully awake to the truth that to profess to see Christianity through the spectacles of a number of second or third rate men who lived in Queen Elizabeth's time (and this is what office-holders under the thirty-nine articles do), men whose works one never dreams of reading for the purpose of enlightening and edifying one's self, is an intolerable absurdity and that it is time to put the formularies of the Church of England on a solider basis."

Of one thing we may be sure, that any increased influence which he might have obtained later would have been used with an honest endeavour to reconcile the working classes to the Church, and to make the gulf which separates them from what is called "society" a little narrower and less perilous. As Professor at Oxford he would doubtless have made substantial contributions to historical and biographical literature, and although he would soon have ceased to be a schoolmaster, he would have continued to exercise great influence as a governor of schools, and as a speaker in conferences, in the pulpit, and possibly in the House of Lords, on subjects connected with the improvement of our public schools. Books on the philosophy or methods of education it was not in him to write, but he would certainly have found means to keep in public view the principles of discipline and instruction which he had sought to exemplify at Rugby. The new claims of the physical sciences for recognition as substantial parts of a system of liberal education in the Universities and public schools would have been received by him with respect, but not with enthusiasm. They would to the last have seemed to him inferior in weight to the older claims of the "humanities" — language, letters, history, and philosophy — to form the staple of a gentleman's education.

Nor can it be doubted that, had his life been prolonged, the later developments of popular instruction would have interested him keenly, on personal as well as on public grounds. His solicitude to extend the blessings of education to the poorer classes was with him a passion, which later events and controversies would have done much to intensify. Kay Shuttleworth, Lord John Russell, William Allen, Lord Lansdowne, and Bishop Stanley of Norwich would have found in him an energetic ally. And none who followed with any care the discussions, in 1870, on the introduction of the Education Act, and who marked the far-seeing and generous spirit in which that measure was conducted through Parliament by Mr. W. E. Forster, the Vice-President of the Council, could fail to be conscious of the happy influence which had descended from Rugby upon that statesman's domestic life. Those of us who were privileged in those days to know the interior of the delightful home at Wharfeside, understood well in how charming and effective a way all that was best in the Arnoldian tradition had helped to shape the convictions and to control the policy of the Minister of Education. Had Arnold lived till 1870, the problem which his son-in-law was called upon to solve would have aroused his enthusiastic interest; and his guidance and encouragement would certainly not have been wanting in the progress of the Bill. The large tolerance which characterized that measure, its sympathy with the aspirations of the working classes for enlightenment and culture, the political insight which it exhibited, and above all the determination of its author to enlist on behalf of a system of National Education the co-operation of good men of various religious creeds, would all have appealed to Arnold's sympathy. There was thus a very real, though at first sight not obvious historical connexion between Thomas Arnold and the memorable Education Act of 1870.

A letter which I have received from the Very Rev. G. D. Boyle, the Dean of Salisbury, sums up with so much truth the impression which Arnold's life and character made upon the generation immediately following him, that it may be fitting to insert it here:

"When Dr. Arnold was suddenly taken away from the work of his great school, I think it was very soon evident from the generous appreciation of his work at Rugby and as a professor at Oxford, that he had really outlived the many severe judgments of his earlier life, and had fully justified the opinion formed of him by the Provost of Oriel,

Dr. Hawkins, when he was a candidate for the head-mastership. All who had been at Rugby under him were never weary in telling of the impression made by his earnest sermons and his lessons in school. But from the moment that Dean Stanley's admirable life appeared, Arnold's influence, hitherto confined to his own pupils, became a moving force in English school life. I remember well how head-masters and under-masters at the old Charterhouse exhorted all senior boys to read the story of Arnold's life and aim at some of the great objects so admirably described by Stanley. The late Dean Howson of Chester, who had seen Arnold very shortly before his death, told me that he thought the contagious enthusiasm of Dr. Arnold's character had been fully represented in Stanley's *Life*. The unfinished Roman History and the Oxford Lectures had an influence of their own. From the time when the rule of Arnold was fully recognized, there was a speedy attempt to introduce greater variety into the course of school lessons. Dr. Moberly told me that he had never known anything like the fire that was kindled by Arnold's educational work. Men, who were far from agreeing with many of Arnold's most cherished beliefs, gathered from his example and method lessons of the deepest importance. Arnold's edition of Thucydides enabled many, for the first time, to realize the true connexion between ancient history and modern political life. His generous estimate of Mitford's *Greece* in his Oxford Lectures, and his hearty delight in Carlyle's *French Revolution*, made many a reader feel that there ought to be no divorce between classical studies and the wide acquaintance with modern literature and politics, so often advocated by men like the late Professor Freeman and Dean Stanley. When I first entered the University of Oxford I found there was a disposition on the part of many to undervalue the leading characteristics of Rugby men. It may have been true that Arnold's power was sometimes felt too keenly, and that grave problems, difficult of solution were, at times, approached by young men who had hardly mastered their importance. But when I remember the earnest spirit and love of truth manifested by men like Walter Stirling, John Conington, Thomas Sandars, Henry Smith, Theodore Walrond, and William Bright—alas! the only survivor of that remarkable group —I seem to realize something of the true Arnoldian afflatus."

Here is a somewhat different testimony from another who knew and loved him. In one of Professor Jowett's letters, he says of Arnold: "His peculiar danger was not knowing the world and character, — not knowing where his ideas would take other people and ought to take himself. Yet, had he been living, how we would have nestled under his wings!"[1]

There is a small side chapel in Westminster Abbey, the entrance to which is concealed by a huge cliff in the shape of a monument to the memory of Craggs, Addison's colleague as Secretary of State. In this enclosure the seeker may find a group of memorial busts, representing F. D. Maurice, Kingsley, Keble, Wordsworth, and Matthew Arnold. And in 1896 a marble effigy of Thomas Arnold was placed in this congenial company. The ceremony of unveiling was simple, and was appropriately performed by Dean Bradley, himself a former pupil of Arnold at Rugby. More than half a century had passed since Arnold's death, but in that time his fame and influence had steadily grown, and on the following day, July 17, 1896, an accomplished writer in the *Times* gave

[1] Life and Letters of Benjamin Jowett, by E. Abbott and L. Campbell.

expression to the national sentiment in words which well deserve to be reproduced here.

"No one made a deeper change in education, a change which profited those who had never been at a public school. As much as any one who could be named, Arnold helped to form the standard of manly worth by which Englishmen judge and submit to be judged. A man of action himself, he sent out from Rugby men fit to do the work of the world. The virtues which his favourite Aristotle extolled — courage, justice, and temperance — were his, and the influence of his character and teaching was calculated to make brave, high-minded soldiers, zealous enlightened clergymen, lawyers with a just sense of the nature of their vocation, and useful and public-spirited members of the State. The width and range of his teaching are apt to be forgotten by those who dwell on his personal influence. If he offered no large interpretation of life, if in his writings there are rarely 'thoughts beyond the reaches of the soul,' if as an historian he seems more at home in dealing with the geographical aspects of his subject, or in clear delineation of the movements of events, than in discovering the hidden springs of action, if he never or rarely let fall a pregnant unforgettable word, he had conceptions, new in his time, first and foremost his lofty conception of education, his conception of the Church as a great agency of social amelioration, his idea of each citizen's duty to the State, his view of history as a whole, with no real division between ancient and modern, the interest, new in his time, which he felt in the elevation of the masses. One must have been at Rugby or Oxford in the thirties to appreciate the effect of Arnold's sermons on generous, susceptible youth. Even in the volume of national life as it flows to-day, there may be detected the effect of the pure, bracing stream which long ago joined it."

CHAPTER VIII

Matthew Arnold — The materials for his biography — His wishes — The main facts of his life — His letters — His character — His inspectorship — Distaste for official routine — His relations to managers — A school manager's recollections — The office of a School Inspector — Its opportunities of influence — The Revised Code — Arnold's methods of work — Testimony of his assistant

DR. ARNOLD'S eldest son, Matthew, has since occupied a larger space in the eyes of his contemporaries than the father had ever filled. He is known to the world as a *litterateur* of singular charm and insight, as a poet of unquestioned genius, and as one who criticised with keenness, but with a delicate and playful humour all his own, the literature, the social life, the religious world, and the political events of his day. In all these respects his career and influence differed substantially from those of his father. During thirty-five years of his life his official position was that of an Inspector of Schools, and the influence he exerted on public education was necessarily large. None hated more heartily than he the hybrid word "educationist," or would sooner have disavowed it as a designation for himself; but it was as an educationist that a large section of the public insisted on regarding him, and it is with his share in the history of public instruction, and in the formation of public opinion upon it, that we are here chiefly concerned.

It was his express wish that he might not be made the subject of a biography. That wish has been respected by his surviving relatives, and implies an equally binding obligation upon all those who knew and loved him. But it has not been held by those most competent to judge to be a reason for withholding the publication of a selection of his letters, which form, in fact, an autobiography. The two volumes of letters, published in 1895 under the skilful and sympathetic editorship of Mr. George Russell, cover, in fact, the whole period of Arnold's activity, from 1848 to the end of his life, and disclose as fully as any biography could do the main incidents of his career. From these volumes, from official reports which are *publici juris*, and from his numerous writings, aided in some small degree by my personal recollections of a colleague during nearly thirty years, it is not difficult to attempt some estimate of the influence which he exerted on his generation.

He was born in 1822, at Laleham, his father being then, as we have already seen, a clergyman without a benefice, occupied in preparing young pupils for the University. In 1836 he was sent to Winchester, the school of which his father always retained grateful recollections, the head master being Dr. Moberly, afterwards Bishop of Salisbury. In the following year he was removed to Rugby, where he lived in his father's house. In 1840 he won an open scholarship at Balliol, and in 1841 a school exhibition. During his residence at Oxford he succeeded in obtaining the

Hertford scholarship and the Newdigate prize for his poem on Cromwell. One who knew him well, and was his constant companion at Oxford, said of him in those days: "His perfect self-possession, the sallies of his ready wit, the humorous turn which he could give to any subject that he handled, his gaiety, exuberance, versatility, audacity, and unfailing command of words, made him one of the most popular and successful undergraduates that Oxford has ever known." He took his degree in the Second Class in the Final Classical Schools in 1844, and obtained a fellowship at Oriel in the following year, just thirty years after the election of his father. Among his colleagues at Oriel were Dean Church, Dean Burgon, Fraser afterwards Bishop of Manchester, Buckle afterwards Canon of Wells, Earle afterwards Professor of Anglo-Saxon, and Arthur Hugh Clough.

After leaving Oxford, there was a brief period in which he assisted in the classical teaching at Rugby, and he was then appointed private secretary to the Marquis of Lansdowne, the Lord President of the Council in 1847. In 1851 Lord Lansdowne offered him an Inspectorship of Schools under the Privy Council, and in the same year he married Frances, daughter of Mr. Justice Wightman. This post he held up to the year 1886, when he retired from the public service. But on three several occasions, as we shall see hereafter, he was detached from the regular duties of the inspectorship for special services, and inquiries into the state of education in foreign countries. Of the public duties which he undertook outside that of the Council Office, the most important were the Professorship of Poetry at Oxford, which he held during two periods of five years each, from 1857 to 1867, and the lecturing tour he undertook in America in 1883. He did not long survive his retirement from the public service, but died suddenly on the 15th of April, 1888, a victim to an affection of the heart not unlike that which had proved fatal to his father and grandfather.

The two volumes of letters,[1] from which these facts can be gleaned, have been edited with judicious and pious care by Mr. George W. E. Russell. They will hardly add much to Arnold's *literary* reputation; and, interesting as they are, they do not suffice to place him in the ranks of the great letter-writers. The peculiar charm which has in different ways given to the epistles of Cicero, of Erasmus, of Pope, of Cowper, of Madame de Sévigné, of Chesterfield, of Charles Lamb, and of Byron their right to a permanent place in Epistolary literature, can scarcely be said to be possessed by these letters. They were evidently not written with even a remote view to their possible publication. They deal only incidentally and in a small degree with matters of public and historical interest, and they do not, to nearly the same extent as his father's, reveal his more matured and serious views on great questions. They disclose only the *vie intime*, and are addressed mainly to his mother, his wife, sisters, and daughters. Very few of them are

---

[1] Letters of Matthew Arnold, 1848–1888. Collected and arranged by George W. E. Russell.

addressed to public men or colleagues. Letters of this latter kind doubtless exist, and would have added much to the value of the book had the editor felt at liberty to use them. But Mr. Russell, whose own fine insight, his literary gifts, and his affectionate relations with the writer of the letters would have specially qualified him to write a full biography, has treated the wishes of his friend as sacred; and valuable as are the materials which he has collected, they furnish only an inadequate picture of Matthew Arnold's life. Yet that picture is one of singular attractiveness. The letters enable the reader to trace the successive stages of a career of steadily increasing honour and public usefulness. They reveal a tender and home-loving nature, great fortitude under disappointment and losses, remarkable intellectual activity, a keen enjoyment of social life and of foreign travel, strong interest in public events, and an unaffected delight at the reception with which his own writings were welcomed by the reading public, and at the influence and fame which they brought to him.

The letters show also how singularly happy he was in his domestic relations, how mother, wife, sisters, and children were specially gifted with the power to evoke what was best in him, and to cheer and animate his life; and how the memory of his father, who had so early been removed from them, continued to hover over the home, to give a sacredness and dignity to the whole of the family history, and to ennoble the aims of all who were nearly connected with him.

Incidentally, also, the letters disclose features of his character which would otherwise have been less clearly known. His delight in natural scenery, and particularly in flowers, his fondness for pet animals, the avidity with which in his travels he seized upon and appreciated any incidents which threw light on the history or social characteristics of foreign peoples, the patient and thorough study which he devoted to the preparation of any work in which he was engaged,— all stand revealed in his letters, and are all the more clearly visible because of the *naïveté* of these private utterances, so different in many respects from the account he gives of himself in his published writings. As one reads "Arminius," and some of the less serious articles which Arnold wrote, one is apt to regard the writer as an amiable trifler, who wrote easily, and played lightly with the superficial aspect of great questions. But the reader of his letters will see that every lecture he delivered and every article he wrote was a real task to him, and was carefully thought out and finished.

One learns also in his letters from abroad, as in those of his father, that he seems to be very little attracted by what are called the fine arts. He is impressed by the Duomo of Florence, and by the splendour and historical associations of that beautiful city; but of the pictures in the Uffizi and the Pitti Gallery, or indeed of any art collection in Europe, he has hardly a word to say. Sculpture, painting, and architecture do not arouse in him the critical faculty. Nor did the modern triumphs of inventiveness and enterprise in the application of science affect him much. Every man who is good for anything has limitations to his tastes and sympathies; and it is interesting to notice all through his letters the supreme place which letters, philosophy, and history occupied in his ideal of human development and culture, and the comparatively low place he assigned to material interests and progress.

Another limitation, less pleasant to dwell upon, becomes very manifest as the reader makes the personal acquaintance of the writer of these familiar and charming letters. He speaks constantly of his official work in terms which show that it was distasteful to him, and that he regarded it as drudgery; *e.g.* "It is a long, tedious business hearing the students give specimen lessons at the Training Schools. There is little real utility in it and a great deal of claptrap, and that makes the expenditure of time the more disagreeable to me. However, I get a good many notes written, and odds and ends of things done."[1] Throughout the letters appear constant references to his official work as uncongenial and wearisome. It was not a profession he would have chosen had he been free to choose. When Lord Lansdowne offered him the post, he accepted it, as he used frankly to say afterwards, because he wished to marry, and because an assured income was necessary for him. Having, however, been appointed to the office, he conscientiously sought to perform its

[1] Letter, Nov. 15, 1870.

duties, and at first he expected to find the work more interesting than it proved to be.

"I think," he said, "I shall get interested in the schools after a little time; the effects on the children are so immense, and their future effects in civilizing the next generation of the lower classes who, as things are going, will have most of the political power of the country in their hands, may be so important. It is really a fine sight in Manchester to see the anxiety felt about them, and the time and money the heads of the cotton manufacturing population are willing to give them. In arithmetic, geography, and history the excellence of the schools I have seen is quite wonderful, and almost all the children have an equal amount of information; it is not confined, as in schools of the richer classes, to the one or two cleverest boys."

As time went on, however, his official work became less attractive than he had hoped to find it. In 1854, in a letter to his mother, he says: "I more and more have the feeling that I do not do my inspecting work really well and satisfactorily, but I have also had a stronger wish than usual not to vacillate and be helpless, but to do my duty, whatever that may be; and out of that wish one may always hope to make something." When the proposal was made to him in 1859 that he should go out as Foreign Commissioner, the relief was peculiarly welcome to him. "You know," he writes to his sister, "that I have no special interest in the subject of public education, but a mission like this appeals even to the general interest which every educated man cannot help feeling in such a subject. I shall for five months get free from the routine work of it, of which I sometimes get very sick, and be dealing with its history and principles."[1]

Again, in 1862, he writes: "I sometimes grow impatient of getting old amidst a press of occupations and labour for which, after all, I was not born. The work I like is not very compatible with any other. But we are not here to have facilities found us for doing the work we like, but to make them." When superintending the business of making out statistical returns in 1871, with a view to setting the Education Act in motion, he was supplied with an assistant, of whom he says:

"He has done his work very well and likes all the bustle and the business of communicating with school managers, and they also like to be communicated with. I like to set my man in motion, lay out for him the range of the information I want, suffer him to get it in his own way and at whatever length best suits him and the managers, hear his story and often decide on the recommendation to be made. There are a few points of real difficulty sometimes in making a recommendation, and here I think I am useful. There is no difficulty in all the rest; others can do it quite as well as I can, and I am glad not to spend myself upon it. It is, however, what I have generally been spent upon for the last twenty years so far as public education is concerned."[2]

This extract is characteristic, for, while it shows his real interest in any question where principle or policy was concerned, it also betrays his repugnance

[1] Letter, Feb. 16, 1859.
[2] Letter, Nov. 28, 1871.

to the mere details of official administration. Hearing the lessons of students of the Training Colleges, and estimating their goodness or badness, for example, appeared to him the most wearisome drudgery. Here is a playful sketch of his inspectorial work:

"I must go back to my charming occupation of hearing students give lessons. Here is my programme for this afternoon: Avalanches, the Steam Engine, the Thames, Indian Rubber, Bricks, the Battle of Poictiers, Subtraction, the Reindeer, the Gunpowder Plot, the Jordan. Alluring, is it not? Twenty minutes each, and the days of one's life are only threescore years and ten!"

Under all these playful yet half-pathetic grumblings, there was concealed more of real interest in the duties of his office than he actually acknowledged. And, in truth, it may be doubted if any other laborious and responsible post in the public service would have suited him better. A secretaryship, or any office which condemned him to sit for six hours a day at a desk, minuting documents and "having the honour to be," would have proved intolerable to him. The inspectorship, at least, offered him more freedom, more variety, greater power of adjusting his duties to his own convenience, and, it must be owned, in his case at least, larger leisure for literary pursuits than he could have otherwise obtained. Like Charles Lamb, John Mill, and Henry Taylor, he chafed occasionally under the restraints of official routine. But on the whole the public has dealt indulgently with those of its servants who have reflected lustre on official life by the repute they have gained in the world of letters; and Arnold was always ready to acknowledge that he had been permitted to bear the yoke lightly, and that his colleagues and official superiors, who were all proud of him, did their best to relieve him from work which he disliked.

It is needless to say that his visits to managers were peculiarly welcome, on personal grounds, and that incidentally, though without any show of official authority, he often helped them much in showing the direction which their own efforts ought to take. For example, the Dean of Salisbury, in his interesting *Recollections*, speaks warmly of the intense refreshment and pleasure he had when Matthew Arnold came to inspect a school at Kidderminster.

"I once," he adds, "heard a famous preacher at Oxford compare a student's first acquaintance with Bengel's *Commentary* to the admission of a ray of light when a shutter was opened in a darkened room. The arrival of Matthew Arnold at my lodgings was something like this. He brought with him a complete atmosphere of culture and poetry. He had something to tell of Sainte-Beuve's last criticism, some new book like Lewes' *Life of Goethe* to recommend, some new political interest to unfold, and, in short, he carried you away from the routine of every-day life with his enthusiasm and his spirit. He gave me most valuable advice as to the training of pupil teachers. 'Open their minds,' he would say, 'take them into the world of Shakespeare, and try to make them feel that there is no book so full of poetry and beauty as the Bible.' He had something to tell me of Stanley and Clough, and it is really difficult to say what a delightful tonic effect his visits produced. . . . One of his pleasantest characteristics was his perfect readiness to discuss with complete command of temper, views and opinions of his own which he knew I did not share and thought dangerous. All who knew him constantly regretted that a man of such wonderful gifts should have to spend his life in the laborious duties of a School Inspector."[1]

To Dr. Boyle, as a school manager, naturally anxious about the record of "passes" and the amount of the government grant, the School Inspector was apt to seem a state functionary only, a hardened official, condemned to routine and absorbed in the mechanical duty of examining young children and in filling up schedules and returns. But neither he nor any of Arnold's many admirers, who used to describe his work as that of one "cutting blocks with a razor," ever took due heed of the manifold interests with which a School Inspector comes in contact, or the many opportunities which his office presents of public usefulness and intellectual influence.

And it must be owned that Arnold himself hardly realized the value of such opportunities or the importance of the functions which he was called on to discharge. Every official post in the world has in it possibilities which are not easily visible to the outside critic, and which cannot be measured by the merely technical requirements laid down by authority. And this is true in a very special sense of such an office as Inspector of Schools, when the holder of the office likes and enjoys his work and seeks *ampliare*

---

[1] *Recollections of Dean Boyle*, p. 180.

jurisdictionem, and to turn to the most beneficial use the means at his command and the authority which his office gives. His first duty, of course, is to verify the conditions on which public aid is offered to schools, and to assure the Department that the nation is obtaining a good equivalent for its outlay. But this is not the whole. He is called upon to visit from day to day schools of very different types, to observe carefully the merits and demerits of each, to recognize with impartiality very various forms of good work, to place himself in sympathy with teachers and their difficulties, to convey to each of them kindly suggestions as to methods of discipline and instruction he has observed elsewhere, and to leave behind him at every school he inspects some stimulus to improvement, some useful counsel to managers, and some encouragement to teachers and children to do their best. There are few posts in the public service which offer larger scope for the beneficial exercise of intellectual and moral power, or which bring the holder into personal and influential relations with a larger number of people. It will be an unfortunate day for the Civil Service if ever the time comes when an office of this kind is regarded as one of inferior rank, or is thought unworthy of the acceptance of men of high scholarship and intellectual gifts. To hundreds of schools in remote and apathetic districts, the annual visit of an experienced public officer, conversant with educational work and charged with the duty of ascertaining how far the ideal formed at headquarters and under the authority of Parliament has been fulfilled, is an event of no small importance. And it matters much to the civilization of the whole district whether this duty is entrusted to pedants and detectives who confine their attention to the routine of examination, or to men whose own attainments command respect, and who are qualified by insight, enthusiasm, and breadth of sympathy to advise local authorities, and to form a just judgment both of the work of a school and of the spirit in which the work is done. He whose own thoughts and tastes move habitually on the higher plane is the best qualified to see in true perspective the business of the lower plane, and to recognize the real meaning and value of the humblest detail.

> "For most men in a brazen prison live,
> Where in the sun's hot eye,
> With heads bent o'er their toil, they languidly
> Their lives to some unmeaning task-work give,
> Dreaming of nought beyond their prison wall.
> And as year after year
> Fresh products of their barren labour fall
> From their tired hands, and rest
> Never yet comes more near,
> Gloom settles slowly down over their breast;
> And while they try to stem
> The waves of mournful thought by which they are prest,
> Death in their prison reaches them
> Unfreed, having seen nothing, still unblest." [1]

This was not an ideal of life which satisfied Arnold. But I am unable to agree with those who think his

[1] A Summer Night.

great gifts were thrown away upon a thankless and insignificant office. It is true, he regarded many of its duties as mere task-work, and that he reserved the best of himself for literary and other employments more congenial to him. But it is also true that his influence on the schools was in its own way far more real and telling than he himself supposed. Indirectly, his fine taste, his gracious and kindly manner, his honest and generous recognition of any new form of excellence which he observed, all tended to raise the aims and the tone of the teachers with whom he came in contact, and to encourage in them self-respect and respect for their work.

From the official point of view, he was not, it must be owned, an exacting Inspector. If he saw little children looking good and happy, and under the care of a kindly and sympathetic teacher, he would give a favourable report, without inquiring too curiously into the percentage of scholars who could pass the "standard" examination. He valued the elementary schools rather as centres of civilization and refining influence than as places for enabling the maximum number of children to spell and write, and to do a given number of sums without a mistake. Hence he was never in sympathy with the drastic and revolutionary policy recommended by the Duke of Newcastle's Commission in 1861, under which the only measure of the efficiency of a school was to be the number of "passes" in reading, writing, and arithmetic it could contrive to score. This policy was afterwards known as "Payment by Results," and was adopted by Parliament at the instance of Mr. Robert Lowe, then Vice-President of the Council, who defended the principle with great ability, and who embodied it pitilessly and in its most unqualified form in the celebrated Revised Code of 1862. Arnold was willing to admit that the application of this rather wooden and statistical test to school work really protected a great many of the less promising scholars from neglect, and brought up a larger number of them than before to a certain level of proficiency in the mere rudiments of instruction. But he never ceased to complain that the system tended to encourage mechanical and unintelligent methods of teaching, to leave out of view the best results of intellectual discipline and moral training, and to lower the conception of teachers in regard to the true office and work of a good school. There can be no doubt that the Revised Code did much to increase his distaste for his official duty and to make him feel that he was working under unfavourable conditions. It will be seen hereafter that when opportunity offered, he showed a frank courage all the more creditable to one whose reports were presented to his official superiors, and that he pointed out with clearness and force the inadequacy of the system and its impoverishing effect on the instruction.

His valued assistant, Mr. Thomas Healing, who wrought with him among the Westminster Schools for several years, thus describes his methods of work:

"I was struck by his perfect frankness and candour in all his educational relationships. He never pretended to be an oracle in methods of instruction, and therefore never attempted to prescribe to teachers the precise methods they should use, though he would often kindly criticise a teacher's mode of handling a subject if it lacked simplicity or breadth of treatment. For example, the multiplication of mere topographical details in geography, neglect to arrange facts in illustration of great general principles, or wandering among points of little practical value in grammar, while the main facts and rules bearing upon the construction of sentences were overlooked. Such errors in method always drew from him an adverse judgment, because he was particularly open to admire logical arrangement, clearness, the marshalling of matter in view of a definite end. But even in such cases he rarely suggested the method that should be adopted. He claimed "free play for the Inspector" and accorded the same to the teacher, being always ready to acknowledge and praise originality of treatment, and to allow him full liberty to give any turn to the instruction for which his special tastes and acquirements qualified him.

"Neither did he pose as a specialist in the matter of school-fittings and architecture. Some of his judgments on these topics, as contained in his reports (*e.g.* the use and abuse of galleries, the Old British tripartite system), are most reasonable and sound; but they are rather the opinions of an educated outsider, speaking from the facts brought under his notice, than of the specialist. He knew and highly esteemed those of his colleagues, who, in these technical matters, could speak with authority.

"In the Elementary Schools he did much to improve the reading books. He complained of many of them as filled 'with the writing of second or third rate authors, feeble, incorrect, and colourless,' or 'with dry scientific disquisitions, which are the worst possible instruments for teaching to read, and which spoil the scholar's taste when they are nearly his only means for forming it.' I happen to know of cases in which books were recast, owing to his influence, and their matter substantially improved.

"Mr. Arnold frequently drew attention to the want of culture in the case of both pupil teachers and Training-College students, as evidenced by their inability to paraphrase a plain passage of prose or poetry, without totally misapprehending it, or falling into gross blunders of taste and expression. He states his opinion that the study of portions of the best English authors and composition might with advantage be made a part of their regular course of instruction to a greater degree than prevailed at the time. His anxiety that the children should feel the refining influence of letters led him, as the best means to attain that end, to promote the higher education of teachers, and especially to direct them to the study of literature. He inspired many a young teacher with the desire to work in the direction of obtaining a London degree, and even those who did not succeed were permanently benefited by the efforts they made. If he found a young man of promise in a school, he generally had with him some serious and sympathetic talk on this subject; and some have told me in the after years that they would never have attempted a work of such difficulty but for the stimulus applied by Mr. Arnold. In the same direction was his advocacy of the teaching of French and Latin to the more advanced scholars. He thought the study of an inflected language would prove helpful in studying grammatical principles, and that Latin would give an insight into the meaning of many English words, and help to widen the vocabulary. His advice in the matter of languages was not taken to any large extent, though something was done; and Mr. Arnold gave an annual prize to be competed for by the pupil teachers of his district in elementary French.

"His ideal of excellence was high. His own eminence in literature, and his earnest belief in the power of letters, as interpreted by himself, to humanize and elevate men and to make them reasonable, led him to take the steps I have indicated for teachers and scholars to come under its influence. In a school, he looked for indications of the operation of this power, as shown in the performance of recitation with due intelligence and expression and, if possible, with feeling; in grammar when marked by accurate thinking and correct application of rules; and in composition by appropriate use of words. He expected that orderly thinking and the habit of stating things clearly should be shown in other subjects of instruction, valuing these excellences far above mechanical accuracy or stores of crude information. Though endowed with deficient musical faculty, he appreciated tasteful singing, and highly estimated its refining influence.

"In striving to arrive at a just estimate of the state of the instruction in a school, he would often examine in elementary subjects the Second Standard, as giving some measure of the accuracy of the spelling and arithmetic; and then the reading, recitation, and grammar of the upper division, thus gauging the extent to which anything approaching culture had penetrated. His usefulness as an Inspector, appears to me, lay very much in his success in bringing some tincture of letters into the curriculum of the Elementary School.

"As an eminent critic and man of letters, possessing a great knowledge of the state of education at home in its broader aspects through a most extensive acquaintance with writers, and with the clergy, the scholastic and legal professions, and a similar familiarity with continental education through his employment on European educational commissions, he brought to the study of all educational problems an enlightened judgment and a power of comparison possible to very few. Consequently, his views and conclusions were such as would in most cases command the assent of the great public of cultured men — of the University and literary class he knew so well."

CHAPTER IX

Arnold as an officer of the Education Department — His official reports — Inspection and examination — Formative studies — Learning of poetry — Grammar — Latin and French in the primary school — Science teaching and Naturkunde — Distrust of pedagogic rules — General aim and scope of an elementary school — The teacher's personal cultivation — Religious instruction — The Bible in the common school — Arnold's attempt at a school reading-book with extracts from Isaiah — The failure of this attempt

MATTHEW ARNOLD's position as an officer of the Education Department was exceptional and, in some respects, unique. When he was first appointed, there was a concordat between the Council Office and the various religious bodies, in virtue of which none but clergymen were charged with the duty of inspecting Church of England schools. In like manner Roman Catholic inspectors were charged with the inspection of Catholic schools. His own duty, therefore, as a lay Inspector, was to visit the schools connected with the British and Foreign School Society, Wesleyan, and other Protestant schools not connected with the Church of England. As these schools were far less numerous than others, the district assigned to him at first was very large, comprising nearly one-third of England. After the Education Act of 1870, the system of denominational inspection was necessarily, and very properly, abandoned; districts became smaller, and the official Inspector was required to visit all the schools which received Government aid in the area assigned to him. From this time his official work became less laborious, and was practically limited to one of the easiest divisions of the metropolis, — the borough of Westminster, — a district so well provided with voluntary denominational schools that for a long time there was in it only one school provided by the London School Board.

As a Chief Inspector he had the nominal supervision of his colleagues in the southeastern Division; but the plans which were adopted under the Vice-Presidency of Mr. Mundella, in 1882, for making this supervision effective, and for co-ordinating and harmonizing the work of the District Inspectors by means of visitation and by conferences with their chief, hardly came to maturity during Arnold's term of office, and practically his opportunities for intercourse with his colleagues were not numerous. He was never actually a member of the well-known Code Committee; for, as it has been said, the details of administration, the framing of syllabuses and schedules, and the laying down of the legal conditions under which the public grant should be assessed and distributed, were tasks not to his mind. But when questions of principle were involved, he was frequently consulted, and we who were his colleagues received from him at times very weighty and practical suggestions. I remember well the discussion when the question arose, "Should the teaching of *English* be a compulsory subject, or should it remain optional, say between geography or elementary science?" On that point he was emphatic. Everything else taught in an elementary school might, he said, be made a matter of memory or routine, but good exercises in the vernacular language, and in the meaning, formation, and right use of words, represented the one kind of knowledge in which "cram" was impossible, and which must, if acquired at all, be gained by an effort of thought. He regarded any system of popular education incomplete which did not provide for instruction in the right use of the mother-tongue, as a condition precedent to the acquisition of all else. He dreaded overloading the curriculum of the elementary school with too numerous or pretentious subjects; and was well content to limit the number of optional subjects which might be selected by a teacher from a list containing geography, history, and various branches of science. But some insight into the grammar and literature of the English language was in his view indispensable, and should, in the higher classes at least, be invariably insisted on.

But the chief means at his disposal for impressing these and other views on elementary education upon the Department, teachers, and managers, and upon the public generally, were his annual reports, which were widely read by persons who seldom cared to consult Blue Books. From 1852 to 1882 these Reports, interrupted only by his occasional employment on foreign service, illuminated the official records of the Committee of Council on Education and attracted much public attention. Much of what he said dealt necessarily with statistics, with changes in the Code, and with matters of ephemeral controversy. But he availed himself of the opportunity which these reports offered to state with some fulness his own views on many subjects of abiding interest, and he has thus contributed to render the future aims of our primary-school system clearer, and to make the work of his successors easier.

For example, he formed from the first a just conception of the duty of the Inspector in respect to the frank and fearless exposure of faults. Very early in his official life, he says:

"An Inspector's first duty is that of a simple and faithful reporter to your Lordships; the knowledge that imperfections in a school have been occasioned, wholly or in part, by peculiar local difficulties, may very properly restrain him from recommending the refusal of grants to that school, but it ought not to restrain him from recording the imperfections. It is for your Lordships to decide how far such imperfections shall subsequently be made public; but that they should be plainly stated to you by the Inspector whom you employ, there can be, I think, no doubt at all. . . .

"A certain system may exist, and your Lordships may offer assistance to schools established under it; but you have not surely, on that account, committed yourselves to a faith in its perfect excellence; you have not pledged yourselves to its ultimate success. The business of your Inspector is not to make out a case for that system, but to report on the condition of public education as it evolves itself under it, and to supply your Lordships and the nation at large with data for determining how far the system is successful. If, for fear of discouraging voluntary effort, Inspectors are silent respecting the deficiencies of schools, respecting the feeble support given to one school, the imperfect accommodations in another, the faulty discipline or instruction in a third, and the failure of all alike to embrace the poorest class of children, — if everything is represented as hopeful and prosperous, lest a manager should be disappointed or a subscriber estranged, — then a delusion is prolonged in the public mind as to the real character of the present state of things, a delusion which it is the very object of a system of public inspection exercised by agents of the Government on behalf of the country at large to dispel and remove. . . .

"It is an ungrateful task to seem to deprecate, under any circumstances, consideration and indulgence. But consideration and indulgence, the virtues of the private man, may easily become the vices of the public servant."[1]

Lest, however, the teachers should think his criticisms implied harshness or want of sympathy, he added:

"No one feels more than I do how laborious is their work, how trying at times to the health and spirits, how full of difficulty even for the best; how much fuller for those, whom I too often see attempting the work of a schoolmaster, men of weak health and studious habits, who betake themselves to this profession as affording the means to continue their favourite pursuits. . . . Still, the quantity of work actually done at present by teachers is immense; the sincerity and devotedness of much of it is even affecting; they themselves will be the greatest gainers by a system of reporting which clearly states what they do, and what they fail to do, not one which drowns alike success and failure, the able and the inefficient, in a common flood of vague approbation."

His conception of the Inspector's duty caused him, as we have already said, to view with extreme dis-

[1] Report to the Committee of Council, 1854.

favour that change in the character of school examinations which was a necessary sequel to the Revised Code. He thought that the adoption of a lower and less intelligent standard of excellence in the schools implied and rendered necessary a lowering in the Inspector's office, and he thus contrasted the older system, which estimated the work of a school by inspection, with the newer system of formal individual examination.

"Inspection under the old system meant something like the following: The Inspector took a school class by class. He seldom heard each child in a class read, but he called out a certain number to read, picked at random, as specimens of the rest; and when this was done he questioned the class with freedom, and in his own way, on the subjects of their instruction. As you got near the top of a good school, these subjects became more numerous; they embraced English grammar, geography, and history, for each of which the Inspector's report contained a special entry, and the examination then often acquired much variety and interest. The whole life and power of a class, the fitness of its composition, its handling by the teacher, were well tested; the Inspector became well acquainted with them, and was enabled to make his remarks on them to the head teacher, and a powerful means of correcting, improving, and stimulating them was thus given. . . .

"The new examination groups the children by its standards, not by their classes; and however much we may strive to make the standards correspond with the classes, we cannot make them correspond at all exactly. The examiner, therefore, does not take the children in their own classes. The life and power of each class, as a whole, the fitness of its composition, its handling by the teacher, he therefore does not test. He hears every child in the groups before him read, and so far his examination is more complete than the old inspection. But he does not question them; he does not, as an examiner under the rule of the six standards, go beyond the three matters, — reading, writing, and arithmetic, — and the amount of these three matters which the standards themselves prescribe. Indeed, the entries for grammar, geography, and history have now altogether disappeared from the forms of report furnished to the Inspector. The nearer, therefore, he gets to the top of the school, the more does his examination in itself become an inadequate means of testing the real attainments and intellectual life of the scholars before him. Boys who have mastered vulgar fractions and decimals, who know something of physical science and geometry, a good deal of English grammar, of geography, and history, he hears read a paragraph, he sees write a paragraph, and work a couple of easy sums in the compound rules or practice. As a stimulus to the intellectual life of the school — and the intellectual life of a school is the intellectual life of its higher classes — this is as inefficient as if Dr. Temple, when he goes to inspect his fifth form at Rugby, were just to hear each boy construe a sentence of delectus, conjugate one Latin verb, and decline two Greek substantives. . . . The whole school felt, under the old system, that the prime aim and object of the Inspector's visit was, after insuring the fulfilment of certain sanitary and disciplinary conditions, to test and quicken the intellectual life of the school. The scholars' thoughts were directed to this object, the teachers' thoughts were directed to it, the Inspectors' thoughts were directed to it. . . . The new examination is in itself a less exhausting business than the old inspection to the person conducting it, and it does not make a call as that did upon his spirit and inventiveness; but it takes up much more time, it throws upon him a mass of minute detail, and severely tasks hand and eye to avoid mistakes."[1]

[1] General Report for 1863.

Arnold always insisted on the necessity of including in the course of even the elementary school some ingredients which, though they might have no visible and immediate bearing on the industrial career of the pupil, were what he called "formative." "Sewing, calculating, writing, spelling," he said, "are necessary; they have utility, but they are not formative. To have the power of reading is not in itself formative." Hence he urged the importance of better reading-books. He admitted that for the mere attainment of the mechanical art of reading, the common reading-book, with its promiscuous variety of contents, was well enough. But as literature, as means of forming the taste and judgment of the pupil, they were contemptible. He had a special horror of that "somewhat terrible character, the scientific educator," who wanted to make school reading-books the vehicles for imparting stores of scientific, geographical, and other information. "Good poetry, however," he said, "is formative; it has, too, the precious power of acting by itself and in a way suggested by nature." Hence he always urged the importance of learning choice extracts of poetry. Learning by heart is often called disparagingly learning by rote, and is treated as an old-fashioned, unintelligent exercise and a waste of time. But he attached great value to this exercise.

"I believe that even the rhythm and diction of good poetry are capable of exercising some formative effect, even though the sense be imperfectly understood. But of course the good of poetry is not really got unless the sense of the words is thoroughly learnt and known. Thus we are remedying what I have noticed as the signal mental defect of our school children — their almost incredible scantiness of vocabulary." [1]

Even this counsel of perfection was capable, as he afterwards found, of being interpreted in an unsatisfactory way. Fragments of long poems, such as Scott's *Lady of the Lake*, and other narratives, were often selected, and as these fragments had no unity of their own, and were learned by those who had never read the poems as a whole, the acquisition appeared to him to be very worthless. The experience of one of our colleagues, who reported that on asking the children of an upper class, "Who Shakespeare was," he received for answer that he was a writer of the time of Elizabeth and the author of two works, *Hubert and Arthur* and the *Trial Scene at Venice*, illustrates well the mischievous effect of the common practice in dealing with fragments of great literary masterpieces. He always urged that scholars who offered to recite one or two hundred lines should be made to show that they knew something about the contents of the poem of which the extract formed a part, and should at least have read it through as a whole, and seen the relation in which that extract stood to the rest. He then lays down the conditions which should be observed in the selection of passages for the *memoriter* exercise.

[1] Report for 1878.

"That the poetry chosen should have real beauties of expression and feeling, that these beauties should be such as the children's hearts and minds can lay hold of, and that a distinct point or centre of beauty and interest should occur within the limits of the passage learned — all these are conditions to be insisted on. Some of the short pieces by Mrs. Hemans, such as *The Graves of a Household*, *The Homes of England*, *The Better Land*, are to be recommended because they fulfil all three conditions; they have real merits of expression and sentiment; the merits are such as the children can feel, and the centre of interest, these pieces being so short, necessarily occurs within the limits of what is learnt. On the other hand, in extracts taken from Scott or Shakespeare, the point of interest is not often reached within the hundred lines which is all that children in the Fourth Standard learn."[1]

Of the claims of grammar to be included, even in an elementary school course, he says:

"I attach great importance to grammar, as leading the children to reflect and reason, as a very simple sort of logic, more effective than arithmetic as a logical training, because it operates with concretes or words instead of with abstracts or figures. . . . Parsing is the very best portion of the discipline of grammar, and it is not too hard for Fourth Standard children if it is taught judiciously. The analytic character of our language enables a teacher to bring its grammar more easily within a child's reach; and advantage should be taken of this analytic character, instead of teaching English grammar, as was the old plan, with a machinery borrowed from the grammar of synthetic languages. I am glad to observe that in the instruction of pupil teachers, the analytic method of parsing is coming into use more and more. . . .

[1] Report for 1880.

"I have never been able to understand the contempt with which what is even now effected in grammar in our schools is regarded. The grammar required for the lower standards is spoken of as quite ridiculously insufficient. Yet, is it so insignificant a mental exercise to distinguish between the use of *shelter* in these two phrases, 'to shelter under an umbrella,' and 'to take shelter under an umbrella'? I do not think so; and this is the sort of elementary logic which the grammar for the Second Standard demands, which the children attain to, and which does them, in my opinion, a great deal of good."[1]

It is the belief of some modern writers that Latin and French are subjects of secondary and higher instruction only, and that any attempt to include them in the primary course is an encroachment on the proper province of the intermediate or higher school. That was not Arnold's opinion. He thought that the rudiments of one of those languages, at least, might with advantage be taught to the more advanced scholars even in the elementary school, as a preparation for the right use of any further educational opportunities they might enjoy after leaving that school. And even if no such opportunity occurred, he deemed it essential that the scholar should at least be made aware that there were other languages than his own, and should find what Bacon calls an "entrance" into one of them.

"Every one is agreed as to the exceptional position of Latin among the languages for our study. Our school-boy of thirteen will do little with his rudiments of Latin unless he carries on his education beyond the scope of our elementary schools and their programmes. But, if he does carry it on beyond that scope, Latin is almost a necessity

[1] Report for 1878.

for him. By allowing Latin as a special subject for a certain number of scholars in our elementary schools, we are but recognizing that necessity, and recognizing, as surely we very properly may, that for some of the better scholars in our schools the necessity will arise. French, too, has a special claim. To know the rudiments of French has a commercial value. A boy who is possessed of them has an advantage in getting a place. He knows this himself, and his parents know it; a little French in addition to good attainments in reading, writing, and arithmetic, is a recommendation for a place. A little Latin is not, a little German is not, a little botany is not; a little French is. Here is a reason for admitting French to our list of extra subjects, closely limited though this list ought to be. French has the educational value for our school children of being a second language; it has also an educational value for us from its precision and lucidity — qualities in which the expression of us English people is often deficient; and it is, besides, a matter of instruction which has the advantage of much commending itself to the minds of our scholars themselves and of their parents as a help to a boy's start in life."

Although Arnold thought the demands made for more of science teaching in schools were being unduly pressed, he recognized the need of such teaching within certain limits. He thought that the inclusion of mathematics, animal physiology, physical geography, and botany in the list of optional specific subjects for the primary school was a mistake. But what the Germans called *Naturkunde*, and Professor Huxley called Physiography, — an elementary knowledge of the facts and laws of nature, — appeared to him a necessary ingredient in the primary-school course. For children of thirteen, he thought it premature to enter upon the technicalities of specific sciences.

"The excuse for putting most of these matters into our programme is that we are all coming to be agreed that an entire ignorance of the system of nature is as gross a defect in our children's education as not to know that there ever was such a person as Charles the First. . . . We ought surely to provide that some knowledge of the system of nature should form part of the regular class course. Some fragments of such knowledge do in practice form part of the class course at present. Children in learning geography are taught something about the form and motion of the earth, about the causes of night and day, and the seasons. But why are they taught nothing of the causes, for instance, of rain and dew, which are, at least, as easy to explain to them, and not less interesting? And this is what the teaching of *Naturkunde*, or natural philosophy (to use the formerly received, somewhat over-ambitious English name for the same thing), should aim at; it should aim at systematizing for the use of our schools a body of simple instruction in the facts and laws of nature, so as to omit nothing which is requisite, and to give all in right proportion. Of course the best agency for effecting this would be a gifted teacher; but as gifted teachers are rare, what we have most to wish for is the guidance of a good text-book. Such a text-book does not at present, so far as I know, exist; some man of science, who is also a master of clear and orderly exposition, should do us the benefit of providing one. But, meanwhile, there is no reason for delaying the attempt to teach in a systematic way an elementary knowledge of nature. Text-books abound from which a teacher may obtain in separate portions what he requires; there can be no better discipline for him than to combine out of what he finds in them the kind of whole suited to the simple requirements of his classes. Some teachers will do this a great deal better than others, but all will gain something by attempting it; and their classes, too, however imperfectly it is at first often effected, will gain by its being attempted."[1]

What his view was about the degree of formative influence which was to be expected from the study of physical science, apart from general mental cultivation in the humanities, may be well illustrated by the playful comments which occurred to him once when fresh from the perusal of a number of examination papers which had been sent to candidates for the office of teacher, and had included *inter alia* some questions on the play of *Macbeth*.

"At last year's meeting of the British Association, the President of the Section for Mechanical Science told his hearers that in such communities as ours, the spread of natural science is of far more immediate urgency than any other secondary study. 'Whatever else he may know, viewed in the light of modern necessities, a man who is not fairly versed in exact science is only a half-educated man, and if he has substituted literature and history for natural science, he has chosen the less useful alternative.' And more and more pressure there will be, especially in the instruction of the children of the working classes, whose time for schooling is short, to substitute natural science for literature and history as the more useful alternative. And what a curious state of things it would be if every scholar who had passed through the course of our primary schools knew that when a taper burns, the wax is converted into carbonic acid and water, and thought, at the same time that a good paraphrase of *Canst thou not minister to a mind diseased?* was, *Can you not wait upon the lunatic?* The

[1] Report for 1878.

problem to be solved is a great deal more complicated than many of the friends of natural science suppose. They see clearly enough, for instance, how the working classes are, in their ignorance, constantly violating the laws of health, and suffering accordingly; and they look to a spread of sound natural science as the remedy. What they do not see is that to know the laws of health ever so exactly, as a mere piece of positive knowledge, will carry a man, in general, no great way. To have the power of using, which is the thing wished, these data of natural science a man must, in general, have first been in some measure *moralized;* and for moralizing him it will be found not easy, I think, to dispense with those old agents — letters, poetry, religion. So let not our teachers be led to imagine, whatever they may hear and see of the call for natural science, that their literary cultivation is unimportant. The fruitful use of natural science itself depends, in a very great degree, on having effected in the whole man, by means of letters, a rise in what the political economists call the *standard of life.*" [1]

Thus it is because the study of material facts and laws does not necessarily carry the student into any region beyond that study itself, and because the humaner studies can shed a light on everything else which is to become a subject of investigation and thought, that Arnold always insisted on the superiority of the latter studies to the former, as instruments for the formation of character and the regulation of life.

It is observable that for the fulfilment of his own ideal, and for stimulating fresher and healthier intelligence in place of routine and mechanism, he was not

[1] Report for 1878.

disposed to rely much on the scientific study of the theory of education. Books on pedagogy bored him, and he had a suspicion that when relied on too much, they were apt to beget a formalism of their own.

"How," he asks, "is a sensible teacher likely to effect most practical good? Is it by betaking himself to the scientific teachers of pedagogy, by feeding on generalities, by learning that we are to 'disuse rule-teaching, and adopt teaching by principles,' that we are to teach things 'in the concrete instead of in the abstract,' that we are to walk worthy of the doctrine long ago enunciated by Pestalozzi, that 'alike in its order and its methods education must conform to the natural process of mental evolution'?

"The worst of such doctrines is that everything depends upon the practical application given to them, and it seems so easy to give a practical application which is erroneous. The doctrine of Pestalozzi, for instance, may be excellent, and none can say that it has not found ardent friends to accept it and employ it; and the result is that one sees a teacher holding up an apple to a gallery of little children, and saying, 'An apple has a stalk, peel, pulp, core, pips, and juice; it is odorous and opaque, and is used for making a pleasant drink called cider.' In virtue of like theories new methods of spelling, new methods of learning to read, new methods of learning arithmetic are called for. Some of them are ingenious. We must always remember, however, that their apparent conformity to some general doctrine, apparently true, is no guarantee of their soundness. The practical application alone tests this, and often and often a method thus tested reveals unsuspected weakness. Then there is, besides the difficulty of getting new methods which are unfamiliar substituted for old methods which are familiar."

And in summing up the aims and scope of the elementary school of the future, he says:

"The best thing for a teacher to do is surely to put before himself, in the utmost simplicity, the problem he has to solve. He has to instruct children between the ages of four and thirteen; children, too, who have for the most part a singularly narrow range of words and thoughts. He has, so far as secular instruction goes, to give to those children the power of reading, of writing, and (according to the good old phrase) of casting accounts. He has to give them some knowledge of the world in which they find themselves, and of what happens and has happened in it; some knowledge, that is, of the great facts and laws of nature, some knowledge of geography and of history, above all, of the history of their own country. He has to do as much towards opening their mind, and opening their soul and imagination, as is possible to be done with a number of children of their age, and in their state of preparation and home surroundings."[1]

That this last duty of opening the soul and the imagination could not be performed by mere hirelings and pedants, but needed to be entrusted to persons who regarded their own personal cultivation as one of the chief duties of their office, was a constant theme on which he insisted, in conversations with teachers as well as in official reports: "The teacher will open the children's soul and imagination the better, the more he has opened his own; so he will also clear their understanding the better, the more he has cleared his own." With this principle in view, Arnold never lost an opportunity of urging on the younger teachers the need of more thought and literary culture than are represented by the possession of a Government diploma, and nothing pleased him

[1] Report for 1878.

better than to give special encouragement and sympathy to those teachers in his district who, after obtaining their legal certificate, intended to graduate at the London University, or were otherwise making efforts after self-improvement.

"It is among the teachers that the desire for a better culture, and the attainment of it, most shows itself. It shows itself in those in my district by more and more numerous efforts to pass the examinations which the London University, with a wise liberality, makes accessible to so large and various a class of candidates. I gladly seize every opportunity to express the satisfaction which the sight of these efforts gives me. To the able, the ardent, and the aspiring among the young teachers of schools under my inspection, I say: 'Your true way of advancing yourselves, of raising your position, of keeping yourselves alive and alert amidst your trying labours, is there.' And the more the Government certificate comes to be regarded as a mere indispensable guarantee of competency, not as a literary distinction, the better; literary distinction should be sought for from other and larger sources. . . . The rate of general intelligence in schools and pupil teachers depends mainly, of course, upon the rate of general intelligence in the head-teachers. This will depend upon their continuing and extending the cultivation with which they have started. In no way can they so well do this as by working for a definite object, which will give them matters of study definite and, on the whole, well chosen. The schoolmasters of my district know how I have always encouraged them to try the matriculation examination at the London University.[1] . . . I believe that the languages now required for matriculation are Latin and French, with a third language, which may be either German or Greek. Latin, French, and German are an excellent, and by no means over-difficult, study for our young schoolmasters, and the rest of the examination will

[1] Reports for 1863 and 1874.

present nothing but what is comparatively easy to them. It is my strong hope that it will soon become the rule for every young schoolmaster in my district to matriculate at the London University."

In regard to religious instruction, Matthew Arnold desired to apply to the elementary school principles of action very nearly akin to those which his father had exemplified at Rugby and had advocated in regard to popular literature. He knew well that the best religious influences are not those which are produced by the compulsory enforcement of theological dogmas upon young children. Hence he had no sympathy with those of the clergy and the supporters of denominational schools who think all religious training impossible without the teaching of creeds and catechisms, and the enforcement of the distinctive tenets of their respective sects in the common schools. Yet he attached high value, on intellectual as well as on moral and religious grounds, to the teaching of the Bible in such schools. He regretted that the state of religious controversy, and the rivalries of hostile sects, made it necessary for the authors of the Education Act to exclude the subject of religious instruction from the purview of the official inspectors altogether. He thought that in this way there was grave danger lest the Biblical teaching might suffer neglect.

"Let the school managers," he said, "make the main outlines of Bible history, and the getting by heart a selection of the finest Psalms, the most interesting passages from the historical and prophetical books of the Old Testament, and the chief parables, discourses, and exhortations of the New, a part of the regular school work, to be submitted to inspection and to be seen in its strength or weakness like any other. This could raise no jealousies; or, if it still raises some, let a sacrifice be made for them for the sake of the end in view. Some will say that what we propose is but a small use to put the Bible to; yet it is that on which all higher use of the Bible is to be built, and its adoption is the only chance for saving the one elevating and inspiring element in the scanty instruction of our primary schools from being sacrificed to a politico-religious difficulty. There was no Greek school in which Homer was not read; cannot our popular schools, with their narrow range and their jejune alimentation in secular literature, do as much for the Bible as the Greek schools did for Homer?"[1]

With a view to illustrate his own conception of the purpose which the study of the Bible might serve, merely as an instrument of intellectual culture, Arnold wrote, in 1872, a little book which he called a Bible reading for schools. It consisted of the last twenty-seven chapters of Isaiah, and was annotated and explained under the title of *The Great Prophecy of Israel's Restoration*. In the preface he says:

"Why is this attempt made? It is made because of my conviction of the immense importance in education of what is called *letters;* of the side which engages our feelings and imagination. Science, the side which engages our faculty of exact knowledge, may have been too much neglected; more particularly this may have been so as regards our knowledge of nature. This is probably true of our secondary schools and Universities. But on our *schools for the people* (by this good German name let us call them, to mark

[1] **Report for 1869.**

the overwhelmingly preponderant share which falls to them in the work of national education) the power of letters has hardly been brought to bear at all; certainly it has not been brought to bear in excess, as compared with the power of the natural sciences. And now, perhaps, it is less likely than ever to be brought to bear. The natural sciences are in high favour; it is felt that they have been unduly neglected, they have gifted and brilliant men for their advocates, schools for the people offer some special facilities for introducing them; on the other hand, the Bible, which would naturally be the great vehicle for conveying the power of letters into these schools, is withdrawn from the list of matters with which Government inspection concerns itself, and, so far, from attention."[1]

And he proceeds to show that from the nature of the subject good text-books are more common and more possible in science than in literature, and that in classical schools the literary interest is cultivated by Greek and Roman learning, while in elementary schools there was nothing analogous to it.

"Only one literature there is, one great literature for which the people have had a preparation — the literature of the Bible. However far they may be from having a complete preparation for it, they have some; and it is the only great literature for which they have any. Their bringing up, what they have heard and talked of ever since they were born, have given them no sort of conversance with the forms, fashions, notions, wordings, allusions of literature having its source in Greece and Rome; but they have given them a good deal of conversance with the forms, fashions, notions, wordings, allusions of the Bible. Zion and Babylon are their Athens and Rome, their Ida and Olympus are Tabor

[1] *Bible Reading for Schools*, p. 6.

and Hermon, Sharon is their Tempe; these and the like Bible names can reach their imagination, kindle trains of thought and remembrance in them. The elements with which the literature of Greece and Rome conjures, have no power on them; the elements with which the literature of the Bible conjures, have. Therefore I have so often insisted, in reports to the Education Department, on the need, if from this point of view only, for the Bible in schools for the people. If poetry, philosophy, and eloquence, if what we call in one word *letters*, are a power and a beneficent wonder-working power in education, through the Bible only have the people much chance of getting at poetry, philosophy, and eloquence. Perhaps I may here quote what I have at former times said: 'Chords of power are touched by this instruction which no other part of the instruction in a popular school reaches, and chords various, not the single religious chord only.' The Bible is for the child in an elementary school almost his only contact with poetry and philosophy. What a course of eloquence and poetry (to call it by that name alone) is the Bible in a school which has, and can have, but little eloquence and poetry! and how much do our elementary schools lose by not having any such course as part of their school programme! All who value the Bible may rest assured that thus to know and possess the Bible, is the most certain way to extend the power and efficacy of the Bible."[1]

In further vindication of his choice of the final chapters of the book of Isaiah as an exercise for school reading, he goes on to say: "To make a great work pass into the popular mind is not easy, but our series of chapters have one quality which facilitates this passage for them — their boundless exhilaration. Much good poetry is profoundly melancholy; now the

[1] *Bible Reading for Schools*, p. 10.

life of the people is such that in literature they require joy. If ever that 'good time coming' for which they long, was presented with energy and magnificence, it is in these chapters. It is impossible to read them without catching its glow."[1]

In a private letter to me about this little book, he says, "It is the educational side of the question that I particularly care for. It does not much matter whether or no one thing more or less is produced which in literature is happy and brilliant, there is so much of this in literature already; but whether the people get hold of a single thing in high literature, this point of education is of immense matter."

Arnold was not sanguine in reference to the effect of his effort to produce a reading-book for schools, and indeed its reception was very cold, and I have never heard of a school in which the book was used. There is something pathetic, however, in his evident consciousness that the effort would fail, and yet in his faith that his effort would bear fruit in the future.

"For any one who believes in the civilizing power of letters, and often talks of this belief, to think that he has for more than twenty years got his living by inspecting schools for the people, has gone in and out among them, has seen that the power of letters never reaches them at all, and that the whole study of letters is thereby discredited, and its power called in question, and yet has attempted nothing to remedy this state of things, cannot but be vexing and disquieting. He may truly say, like the Israel of the prophet, 'We have not wrought any deliverance in the earth!' and he may well desire to do something to pay his debt to popular education

[1] *Bible Reading for Schools*, p. 35.

before he finally departs, and to serve it, if he can, in that point where its need is sorest, where he has always said its need was sorest, and where, nevertheless, it is as sore still as when he began saying this twenty years ago. Even if what he does cannot be of service at once, owing to special prejudices and difficulties, yet these prejudices and difficulties years are almost sure to dissipate, and the work may be of service hereafter." [1]

Whether or not Arnold succeeded in fulfilling the official ideal of a Government Inspector is a question hardly worth discussing. But he who undertakes his work in the spirit shown in the extracts here made, and has left behind him influence so calculated to ennoble the primary-school teacher, his work, and his aspirations, will ever be entitled to a high place in the annals of the Education Department, as well as in the world of letters.

[1] *Bible Reading for Schools*, p. 12.

CHAPTER X

Matthew Arnold's employment in foreign countries — The Newcastle Commission of 1859 — The Schools Inquiry Commission of 1865 — Special report to the Education Department, 1885 — Democracy — Relation of the State to voluntary action in France and in England — Why Germany interested Arnold less than France — Advantages of State action — The religious difficulty in France — Why a purely secular system became inevitable in that country — A French Eton — Comparison with the English Eton — Endowment under French law — Latin and Greek as taught in French Lycées — Entrance scholarships — Leaving examinations — Instruction in civic life and duties

It will be seen from Matthew Arnold's letters *passim*, how much he enjoyed occasional opportunities of employment in foreign countries. Three such opportunities came to him in the course of his official life, and were especially welcome to him, partly because he was enabled by them to escape from what seemed to him monotonous and wearisome in his regular official duties, and mainly because inquiries into foreign systems, and their relation to the polity and needs and national character of the several countries in which those systems were operative, were especially congenial to him. The first of his special reports was in 1861, to the Commission which was presided over by the Duke of Newcastle, and which had been charged, in 1859, with the duty of inquiring into the state of popular education in England. The Minutes of Council of 1845 had been in full operation for twelve years when the Commission was appointed, and the Government and the nation desired to know what was the actual working of the measure, and whether or not the State was receiving an adequate return for the increasing grants which were made from the Treasury. The Commissioners, however, wisely resolved that their inquiry should not be restricted to our own country, and that it would help them much to learn by way of comparison what had been done in other lands which had enjoyed a larger experience than our own of State action. Accordingly, Arnold was instructed as Foreign Assistant Commissioner to inquire and report in reference to the state of popular education in France, Holland, and Switzerland.

The second occasion on which he was detached from his ordinary work for special foreign service was in 1865, when the Schools Inquiry Commission, under the chairmanship of Lord Taunton, was charged with the duty of reporting on secondary education in England and Wales. Arnold again accepted the office of Assistant Commissioner, and was instructed to report on the systems of education of the middle and upper classes in France, Germany, Switzerland, and Italy.

For the third time he received, in November, 1885, a summons to make a foreign journey. On this occasion it was the Education Department itself which gave him instructions. In view of contemplated legislation, the heads of that department desired to receive more detailed information from Germany, Switzerland, and France, on four specific points, which were thus indicated: Free education; the quality of education; the status, training, and pensioning of teachers; and compulsory attendance and release from school.

Of these three reports, the first and second, after due publication in the Blue Books, were afterwards reprinted as separate books, the first under the title of *The Popular Education of France, with Notices of that of Holland and Switzerland;* and the second under the title of *Schools and Universities on the Continent.* The third appeared only as a parliamentary paper in 1886.

Many of the statistical and other details of these reports are of temporary interest only, and much of the organization which he describes has by this time been modified or superseded. Hence the narrative which these reports furnish — picturesque and suggestive as it is — has now little more than an historical value. But the experience he gained in these memorable visits led him to consider wider questions than those which concerned the administration of educational bureaus, the work of schools, and the success of their methods. For example, when his first report was reprinted in 1861, in a volume no longer bearing the official stamp, he felt free to prefix to it an essay on the true functions of the State in a democratic community. As a contribution to political philosophy, and as a key to many of his later speculations on public questions, this essay will probably rank as one of his best and most thoughtful utterances. He had been profoundly impressed by reading De Tocqueville, and had learned from that acute thinker to estimate the advantages, and at the same time to perceive some of the perils, of a democratic society, particularly as they were exemplified in the United States and in France. De Tocqueville had urged that democracy was inevitable, and, on the whole, desirable, but desirable only under certain conditions, those conditions capable of being realized by care and foresight, but capable also of being missed. Hence the great desideratum was to seek out and devise that form of democracy, which on the one hand most exercises and cultivates the intelligence and mental activity of the majority, and on the other breaks the headlong impulse of popular opinion by delay, rigour of forms, and adverse discussion. "The organization and establishment of democracy on these principles is," as John Stuart Mill has justly said, "the great political problem of our time."[1]

Arnold concluded from his observation and study that forces were at work which made it impossible for the aristocracy of England to conduct and wield the English nation much longer. It is true that they still have in their hands a large share in the administration, and, as Mirabeau said, "*Administrer, c'est gouverner; gouverner c'est regner; tout se reduit la.*" But in Arnold's view this headship and leadership of one class, with the substantial acquiescence of the body of the nation in its predominance and right to lead, were nearly over. There was nothing to lament in this. The fuller development of national life, the reduction of the signal inequalities that characterize the older societies, and the extension to all classes

[1] J. S. Mill, *Dissertations*, Vol. II., p. 58.

of a due sense of individual responsibility and of corporate existence were, in his view, more than compensation for the loss of a certain stateliness and force which belonged to an aristocratic régime. "The power of France in Europe is at this day mainly owing to the completenesss with which she has organized democratic institutions. The action of the French State is excessive, but it is too little understood in England that the French people has adopted this action for its own purposes, has in great measure attained those purposes by it, and owes to having done so the chief part of its influence in Europe. The growing power in Europe is democracy, and France has organized democracy with a certain indisputable grandeur and success." Arnold's first official visit to the Continent left on him a strong impression of the weakness which comes from our insular dread of State action. He recognized the value of voluntary effort and local initiative in English institutions; but he thought we overestimated these things, and that we had much to learn from the organized State systems of foreign lands, especially that of France.

From the first, France interested him more than Germany. Notwithstanding our nearer affinity in race to the Teutonic people, he thought the English community much more closely akin to the French in their history and genius, their love of liberty, their literature, their national aspirations, and their moral ideals. The Germans he was wont to speak of as a "disciplinable and much disciplined people," who had, it is true, received valuable institutions from the ruling classes, but who had shown in their history less spontaneity of national life, and had undergone fewer of the experiences likely to be specially exemplary to Englishmen than our nearest neighbours, the French. Like Heine, that Paladin of the modern spirit, he gave the preference to France rather than to Germany, because "the French as a people have shown more accessibility to ideas, because prescription and routine have had less hold upon them than upon any other people, and because they have shown more readiness to move and to alter at the bidding (real or supposed) of reason. "Englishmen and Frenchmen have alike the same instinctive sense rebelling against what is verbose, ponderous, roundabout, inane, in one word *niais* or silly, in German literature.[1] In his report, Arnold says further, that the "Prussian people, under its elaborate system of education, have become a studious people, a docile people, a well-informed people if you will, but also a somewhat pedantic and somewhat sophisticated people."[2]

Hence there was much, he thought, to be gained if the men of France and England, though diverse in race, yet morally akin, would observe and understand one another better. Of the Englishman and the Frenchman he said: "Neither is likely to have the other's faults, each may safely adopt as much as suits him of the other's qualities. If I were a Frenchman, I should never be weary of admiring the independent

---

[1] *Mixed Essays.*
[2] *Popular Education,* p. 167.

local habits of action in England, of directing attention to the evils occasioned in France by the excessive action of the State; for I should be very sure that, say what I might, the part of the State would never be too small in France, nor that of the individual too large. Being an Englishman, I see nothing but good in freely recognizing the coherence, rationality, and efficaciousness which characterize the strong State action of France, of acknowledging the want of method, reason, and result which attend the feeble State action of England; because I am very sure that, strengthen in England the action of the State as one may, it will always find itself sufficiently controlled." Tracing the habitual jealousy with which the Englishman is wont to regard Government action to the long struggle for religious and political liberty against a dominant aristocratic and ecclesiastical class, Arnold warned his countrymen that, though this jealousy was justifiable once, it was so no longer. "It is not State action in itself which the middle and lower classes of a nation ought to deprecate, it is State action exercised by a hostile class, and for their oppression. From a State action reasonably, equitably, and rationally exercised, they may derive great benefit, greater by the very nature and necessity of things than can be derived from this source by the class above them. For the middle and lower classes to obstruct such action is to play the game of their enemies, and to prolong for themselves a condition of real inferiority."[1]

[1] Introduction to *Popular Education in France*, p. 41.

After describing the College of France and the numerous State establishments which exist in Paris under the general sanction of the Minister of Public Instruction, to wit, the Schools of living Oriental Languages, the *Bureau des Longitudes,* the Polytechnic Military School, the Naval School of Hydrography, the schools of Woodcraft and Agriculture, of Commerce and of Mines, and the Academy of Medicine, he says:

"Public establishments such as these serve a twofold purpose. They fix a standard of serious preparation and special fitness for every branch of employment — a standard which acts on the whole intellectual habit of the country. To fix a standard of preparation is a very different thing, and it is a far more real homage to intelligence and study than to demand — as we have done since the scandal of our old mode of appointment to public functions grew too evident — a single examination by a single Board, with a staff of examiners as the sole preliminary to all kinds of civil employment. Examinations preceded by preparation in a first-rate superior school give you a formed man; examinations preceded by preparation under a crammer give you a crammed man, but not a formed one. . . . A second purpose which such public establishments serve is this: They represent the State, the country, the collective community in a striking, visible shape, which is at the same time a noble and civilizing one, giving the people something to be proud of and which it does them good to be proud of. The State is, in England, singularly without means of civilization of this kind. But a modern State cannot afford to do without them, and the action of individuals and corporations cannot fully compensate for them; the want of them has told severely on the intelligence and refinement of our middle and lower classes. . . . What the State, the collective, permanent nation honours, the people honour; what the State neglects, they think of no great consequence."[1]

This view of the true function of the State is further summarized in another passage which I transcribe from *A French Eton:*

"Is a citizen's relation to the State that of a dependent to a parental benefactor? By no means; it is that of a member in a partnership to the whole firm. The citizens of a State, the members of a society, are really a partnership — '*a partnership,*' as Burke nobly says, '*in all science, in all art, in every virtue, in all perfection.*' Towards this great final design of their connexion, they apply the aids which co-operative association can give them."

In this rather unpopular belief, and in the light of these general principles, Arnold made his foreign inquiries; and his reports may be described as a sustained argument in favour of this thesis, that once secure an enlightened democracy, a community animated by a progressive spirit and noble ideals, it is the part of wisdom to invoke the collective power of the State to give effect to those ideals.

It is from the point of view thus indicated that Arnold's first report is most suggestive. He describes in full the organization of the primary schools, both in their relation to the provincial academies and to the central government, the salaries and status of the teachers, and the course of normal training through which they pass. He is especially careful to do full justice to the "congreganist" schools, which are

[1] Report to the Schools Inquiry Commission of 1865, Chap. VIII.

maintained by religious bodies, and while conforming to certain well-understood conditions respecting the condition of the premises and the qualifications of the teachers, received little aid from the State. Under the administration of Guizot in 1835 an attempt had been made by the State to co-operate with the churches, and to secure that religious instruction should be given in the common schools. Three only of the numerous religious divisions with which we are familiar were recognized by the State, — the Roman Catholic, the Protestant, and the Jewish. In those communes where more than one of the forms of worship thus recognized is publicly professed, each form was to have a separate school. But the Departmental Council had the power to authorize the union in a common school of children belonging to different denominations. Of children thus united, however, the religious liberty was sedulously guarded. It was provided that ministers of each communion should have free and equal access to the school at separate times in order to watch over the religious instruction of members of their own flock.[1] Arnold, in 1860, found this system working, and spoke favourably of its results. But he had his misgivings about its permanence. "The French system," he said, "recognized certain religious divisions in the population, but it does not divide itself in order to meet them. It maintains its own unity, its own impartiality. In their relations with the State, with the Civil Power, all denominations have

[1] *Popular Education in France*, p. 71.

P

to meet upon a common ground. The State does not make itself denominational; the denominations have to make themselves national." It is mainly because the denominations have failed to make themselves national by co-operating with the State on conditions which the State could accept, that in later years all attempts at compromise and co-operation have been abandoned, and France has taken refuge in the absolutely secular system which now prevails.

The history of this failure to secure a ground of common action between the churches and the civil power in France, as it may be traced in Arnold's volume, is not without a deep and special significance for English readers in our own day. To Americans, it is less instructive, for in the United States the delimitation of duty and responsibility between the churches and the State has been from the first more clearly marked; and the secularization of the common school has met with the national approval, not only because it is the only system on which a State system has been found possible, but because it gives to the churches a stronger sense of their own special responsibility, and is not believed to be inimical to the true interests of religion.

In the interval between the first and the second of his foreign missions, he published, at first in the form of a magazine article, and afterwards in that of a little book, the essay under the title of *A French Eton*. It consisted of a description of two French institutions which had specially interested him, though they lay outside the purview of his first commission. One of these was the Lyceum or public secondary school at Toulouse, considered as a type of a class of school to which there is nothing analogous in England. It is attached to a local academy of the first rank, and is founded and maintained by the State with aid from the Department and the Commune, and under the general control of the Minister of Public Instruction in Paris. All the professors had gone through the excellent normal school course, and were duly licensed. There were between three and four hundred students and a separate preparatory institution, *le Petit Collège*, for boys from six to twelve years of age. The programme of studies included Latin and Greek grammar and the French language, the ancient and the vernacular languages being pursued *pari passu* from the first: *e.g.* Phædrus and La Fontaine, Lucian and Télémaque; in the next class Virgil and Xenophon, with Voltaire's *Charles XII.*, then Sallust and Cicero, with Massillon and Boileau; afterwards the Greek tragedians, Plato and Demosthenes, with Bossuet and Montesquieu, while in the sixth or highest form there was a division into two courses, rhetoric and philosophy, to correspond to the direction, literary or scientific, which the studies of the more advanced scholars were to take. The fees are regulated by public authority; for tuition only, from 110 francs to 180 francs a year, and for boarding and instruction, from 800 francs to 900 francs.

"Such may be the cheapness of public-school education, when that education is treated as a matter of public economy to be administered on a great scale with rigid system and exact superintendence in the interests of the pupil and not in the interest of the school keeper. Such a Lyceum is not managed for speculation or profit, for the public is the real proprietor of the Lyceums which it has founded for the education of its youth and for that object only; the directors of the Lyceum are simple servants of the public employed by the public at fixed salaries."

Another school at Sorèze, a village in the department of the Tarn-et-Garonne, attracted his attention as one of the most successful private schools in France, under the direction of the celebrated Dominican father, Lacordaire. The French Government acknowledges the obligation to allow liberty of teaching, but not liberty to incompetence. Hence, even in private religious enterprises of this kind, the director was bound to hold a certificate of probation and a certificate of competency; but for the rest, the Sorèze institution was one in which the venerable director was free to exercise his own religious influence and to try his own experiments. The programme of studies differed little from that of a Lyceum, although Lacordaire deprecated the more pronounced military system of the State schools. But what impressed Arnold most was the generous and high-toned educational aim of the school and the fact that, at a charge a little more than that exacted in the Lycées, there were to be found in France, under the supervision of responsible public bodies, or of the State itself, middle-class institutions of a type not to be met with at home, and he asked:

"Why cannot we have throughout England as the French have throughout France, as the Germans have throughout Germany, as the Swiss have throughout Switzerland, and as the Dutch have throughout Holland, schools where the middle and professional classes may obtain at the rate of from £20 to £50 a year if they are boarders, and from £5 to £15 a year if they are day scholars, an education of as good quality, with as good guarantees of social character and advantages for a future career in the world, as the education which French children of the corresponding class can obtain from institutions like that of Toulouse or Sorèze?"

Arnold did not argue that either of these institutions exactly corresponded to Eton, or could do for English boys all that Eton does. The great public schools of this country had formed the ruling class, and the ruling class had been, mainly through this influence, imbued on the whole with a high, magnanimous, governing spirit. Those institutions had their origin in ancient endowments. But beautiful and remarkable as are many of the aspects under which our system presents itself, this form of public establishment of education with its limitations, its preferences, its ecclesiastical character, its inflexibility, its inevitable want of foresight, had proved, as time rolled on, to be subject to many inconveniences and to many abuses.

He thought that for the class frequenting Eton, the children of luxury, the grand aim should be not to increase the comforts which would make the school more like their own well-equipped homes; but to give them those good things which their birth and rearing are least likely to give them, to give them (besides book learning) the notion of a sort of republican fellowship, the practice of a plain life in common, the habit of self-help. To the middle class the grand aim of education should be to give largeness of soul and personal dignity; and to the lower class — feeling, gentleness, humanity.

The details collected by Arnold from Holland, Belgium, and Switzerland cannot be summarized here. But it is interesting to observe that, much as these countries differed in circumstances, and in the idiosyncrasies of their people, they all served to confirm his general preference, if not for purely State action in regard to public education, at least for some guidance and sense of responsibility on the part of the State, in dealing with individual and local initiative.

"I do not think we can hope in England for municipalities which, like the Dutch municipalities, can in the main safely be trusted to provide and watch over schools, for a population which, like the Dutch population, can in the main safely be trusted to come to school regularly, or for a government which has only to give good advice and good suggestions in order to be promptly obeyed. Even the Government of Holland, however, has regulated popular education by law; even the school-loving people of Holland, so well taught, so sober minded, so reasonable, is not abandoned in the matter of its education to its own caprices. The State in Holland, where education is prized by the masses, no more leaves education to itself than the State in France, where it is little valued by them. It is the same in the other country of which I have described the school system — in Switzerland. Here and there we may have found, indeed, school-rules in some respects injudicious, in some respects extravagant; but everywhere we have found law, everywhere State-regulation."[1]

His report to the Schools Inquiry Commission of 1867 is chiefly interesting because it contains an account of the organization of secondary instruction in France, Germany, Italy, and Switzerland. In each country the institutions and the public laws are of much later date than our own, and are less influenced by mediæval traditions. For example, the report explains the fundamental difference between the law of inheritance, as it prevails in France, and the common law of England, which allows a testator to name trustees with perpetual succession, and to prescribe for all future time the manner in which the usufruct of his estate shall be employed. "These endowments are of far less importance in France than in England. In the first place, the Revolution made a clean sweep of all old endowments which date from an earlier time. In the second place, the French law sets limits to a man's power of disposing of his property, while in England such limits do not exist. In France, by the *Code Napoléon* (Art. 913, and the articles following), if a man leaves one legitimate child, he may dispose of one-half of his property, and no more, away from him; if he leaves two, he may dispose of one-third, and no more; if he leaves more than two, of one-fourth, and no more. If he has no children, a certain proportion of his property is similarly secured to his nearest representatives within certain limits. The amount of property free

[1] *Popular Education in France*, pp. 233, 234.

to be disposed of in benefactions is thus much smaller in France than in England.

"In England a man names an individual to be trustee, or a number of individuals to be trustees, to carry into effect a charitable request, on conditions assigned by him at pleasure. In France this cannot be done. A founder must entrust his bequest for charitable purposes to a *personne civile*, defined as an *être fictif auquel la loi reconnait une partie des droits qui appartiennent aux personnes ordinaires, et qui peuvent reçevoir des liberalités*. Such a *personne civile* must be either a public establishment (for instance, a public hospital, a parish church, a commune) or an establishment of public utility."[1]

Curious information is given in this report respecting the fluctuations of opinion, during a long succession of Ministers of Public Instruction, in reference to the place which the study of ancient languages should hold in liberal education. But, on the whole, Greek and Latin had retained their traditional supremacy. A passage from a letter addressed to Professor Conington from Paris indicates a substantial difference of ideal between English and French teachers.

"Piles of exercise-books are sent to me to look through, and I wish you could see them with me. The Latin verse is certainly very good, but it is clear that Latin and Greek are cultivated almost entirely with a view to giving the pupil a mastery over his own language — a mastery which has always been the great object of intellectual ambition here and which counts for more than a like mastery does with us. Perhaps, because it does not count for so much

---

[1] Report to Commissioners, note to p. 402.

with us, a like mastery is, in fact, scarcely ever attained in England, certainly never at school."[1]

It will be seen that Arnold's attention in these foreign inquiries was more directed to matters of organization, and to the economical and political aspects of the educational problem, than to the details of pedagogic method. Nevertheless, incidentally and occasionally, he dealt with some topics having a special bearing on the interior work of schools and on matters of policy, on which the minds of teachers are not yet wholly made up. Among these we can only refer to two, of which one is the well-worn topic of entrance scholarships by competition.

"The French *lycées*, however, are guiltless of one preposterous violation of the laws of life and health committed by our own great schools, which have of late years thrown open to competitive examinations all the places on their foundations. The French have plenty of examinations, but they put them almost entirely at the right age for examinations — between the years of fifteen and twenty-five when the candidate is neither too old or too young to be examined with advantage. To put upon little boys of nine or ten the pressure of a competitive examination for an object of the greatest value to their parents, is to offer a premium for the violation of nature's elementary laws, and to sacrifice, as in the poor geese fatted for Strasburg pies, the due development of all the organs of life to the premature hypertrophy of one. It is well known that the cramming of the little human victims for their ordeal of competition tends more and more to become an industry with a certain class of small schoolmasters who know the secrets of the process, and who

[1] Letters, Vol. I., p. 264.

are led by self-interest to select in the first instance their own children for it. The foundations are no gainers, and nervous exhaustion at fifteen is the price which many a clever boy pays for over-stimulation at ten; and the nervous exhaustion of a number of our clever boys tends to a broad reign of intellectual deadness in the mass of youths from fifteen to twenty whom the clever boys, had they been rightly developed and not unnaturally forced, ought to have leavened. You can hardly put too great a pressure on a healthy youth to make him work between fifteen and twenty-five; healthy or unhealthy you can hardly put too light a pressure of this kind before twelve."[1]

On another topic, that of leaving examinations *abiturientem examen*, the experience furnished by Germany seemed to Arnold especially valuable. He discusses the use which was made of such an examination by the State as a qualification for the public service. The course followed with the *Realschulen* and with the higher Burgher Schools is thus described:

"For entrance to the different branches of the public service, the leaving certificate of the classical school had, up to 1832, been required. For certain of these branches it was determined, in 1832, to accept henceforth the certificate of the *Realschule* or the higher Burgher School instead of that of the gymnasium. Different departments made their own stipulations: the Minister of Public Works, for instance, stipulated that the certificate of the candidate for the *Bauakademie* (School of Architecture) should be valid only when the candidate's *Realschule* or higher Burgher School had been one of the first class, or with the full number of six classes, and when he had passed two years in each of the two highest classes. I mention a detail of this kind to show the com-

[1] Report, p. 489.

missioners how entirely it is the boy's school and training which the Prussian Government thinks the great matter, and not his examination."[1]

Finally there is appended to the report a copy of the programme on *Législation Usuelle* in the then newly organized *Enseignement Secondaire Spécial* in France, which, as it relates to a department of a citizen's training scarcely yet recognized by English teachers, is specially suggestive to them. Of this programme he says:

"The programme headed *législation usuelle*, giving the outline of a course on the public and private law, and the administrative organization of France, — how the government is composed, what are the functions of its different departments, how the municipalities are constituted, how the army is recruited, how taxes are raised, what is the legal and judicial system of the country, how in the most important relations of civil life, marriage inheritance, holding property, buying, selling, lending, borrowing, partnership, the laws affect the citizen, — this programme in particular seems to me so well composed, both for what it inserts and what it omits, and so suggestive, that I reprint it at the end of this report for the Commissioners' information. The programmes on the legislation of commerce and industry, and on rural, industrial and commercial economy, are also very interesting; but each of these is more particularly designed for a single division of pupils, according to the class of profession to which they are destined; whereas the programme for *législation usuelle* is designed for all, containing what it is important for all alike to know; therefore it is not so easy a programme to prepare, and has a more general interest when prepared."

[1] Report, p. 566.

CHAPTER XI

Arnold's views of English society — The three classes, the Barbarians, the Philistines, the Populace — Characteristics of the Philistine or middle class — Why his diagnosis, though true in the main, was inadequate — The want of culture among Nonconformists — The disabilities under which they had suffered — A sonnet — Illustration of the difference between public schools and private "academies" — Schools for special trades, sects, or professions — Hymns — Effects of his polemic in favour of a system of secondary instruction

MATTHEW ARNOLD never lost an opportunity of exposing with pitiless candour the fallacy of the belief so fondly cherished by the British Philistine, that we are a well-educated people, and that we are likely to remain so, if we give free play to local initiative and private enterprise. On the contrary, he brought forward, as we have seen, an immense mass of facts, personal experiences, and statistics to prove that whereas in Continental countries, in which the education of the middle class is a matter of national concern and State supervision, "that class in general may be said to be brought up upon the first plane, in England it is brought up on the second plane," and he quotes with sorrowful acquiescence the language of a foreign reporter who said, "*L'Angleterre proprement dite est le pays d'Europe où l'instruction est le moins répandue.*"[1] Arnold regarded it as one of the chief aims of his life to disturb our insular self-

---
[1] Preface to *Schools and Universities on the Continent*.

gratulation, and to make English people profoundly discontented with their present provision for intermediate and higher instruction.

He was fond of dividing English society into three classes, — the upper or aristocratic and official class, the middle class, and the working or lower class. The first he playfully characterized as the *Barbarians*, the second as the *Philistines*, and the third as the *Populace*. Of the first of these classes, he always speaks with good-humoured tolerance and with a certain qualified admiration.

"It is the chief virtue of a healthy and uncorrupted aristocracy that it is in general *in the grand style*. That elevation of character, that noble way of thinking and behaving which is an eminent gift of nature to some individuals, is also often generated in whole classes of men (at least when these come of a strong and good race) by the possession of power, by the importance and responsibility of high station, by habitual dealing with great things, by being placed above the necessity of struggling for little things. It may go along with a not very quick or open intelligence, but it cannot well go along with a conduct vulgar and ignoble."[1]

But on the other hand, in the same essay he dwells emphatically on the incapacity of the ruling class for ideas, and traces to this cause the secret of their declining influence and their want of success in modern epochs.

"They can, and often do, impart a high spirit, a fine ideal of grandeur, to the people; thus they lay the foundations of a great nation. But they leave the people still the

[1] *Mixed Essays*.

multitude, the crowd; they have small belief in the power of the ideas which are its life. . . . In one most important part of general human culture — openness to ideas and ardour for them — aristocracy is less advanced than democracy, and to keep the latter under the tutelage of the former would on the whole be actually unfavourable to the progress of the world. At epochs when new ideas are powerfully permeating in a society, and profoundly changing its spirit, aristocracies, as they are in general not long suffered to guide it without question, so are they by nature not fitted to guide it intelligently."[1]

And he quotes with approval from his favourite, De Tocqueville, the remark "that the common people is more uncivilized in aristocratic countries than in others, because there the lowly and the poor feel themselves, as it were, overwhelmed with the weight of their own inferiority."[2]

It is not easy to understand the true nature of Arnold's influence on public education without considering the estimate he formed of the society in which he lived, and the rather merciless view he took of some of our national foibles and weaknesses. In a spirit which reminds us from time to time of Apemantus, of Jacques, of Swift, or of Carlyle, he poses throughout many of his prose writings as the critic and censurer of mankind. He once said of Goethe:

"He took the suffering human race,
   He read each wound, each weakness clear,
  And struck his finger on the place
   And said, '*Thou ailest, here and here!*'"

[1] *Mixed Essays.*
[2] Irish Essays, *The Future of Liberalism.*

In a sense it is true of Arnold that he set himself the like task, and that on the whole he fulfilled it with sureness of touch, with insight and skill, with a pleasant mingling of raillery and persuasiveness, though not with unqualified success. As he looked upon English society, he thought he saw an upper class materialized and frivolous, a middle class vulgarized, and a lower class brutalized.

But while he recognized some compensation for the lack of ideas in the tone of manners and in the public services of the aristocracy, and some corrective for the peculiar vices of democracy in its openness of mind and accessibility to ideas, he reserved for the middle class his severest criticism and his most humorous invective. He called them Philistines. He said of this class, that although with virtues of its own it was "full of narrowness, full of prejudices, with a defective type of religion, a narrow range of intellect and knowledge, a stunted sense of beauty, a low standard of manners, and averse, moreover, to whatever may disturb it in its vulgarity."[1]

"The great English middle class, the kernel of the nation, the class whose intelligent sympathy had upheld a Shakespeare, entered the prison of Puritanism and had the key turned upon its spirit there for two hundred years. '*He enlargeth a nation,*' said Job, '*and straiteneth it again.*' If the lower classes in this country have utterly abandoned the dogmas of Christianity, and the upper classes its practice, the cause lies very much in the impossible and unlovely

[1] Irish Essays, *The Future of Liberalism.*

presentment of Christian dogmas and practice which is offered by the most important part of the nation, the serious middle class, and above all by its Nonconforming portion."[1]

Arnold's own experience had brought him into exceptionally near contact with this portion of our social organism. As Inspector, during many years, of schools not connected with the Church of England, he was necessarily the recipient of the hospitality of the managers of such schools. He had known what it was to be prayed for by name, and to have his faults gently hinted at in the family devotions. He railed at "the hideousness, the immense ennui of the life which the Puritan type had created." He described the middle-class Londoner as oscillating between a dismal and illiberal life at Islington and an equally dismal and illiberal life at Camberwell. To him the typical Philistine was one who never admired or even knew what was best in literature, but only that which is flimsy and ephemeral; who prided himself on upholding the "dissidence of dissent, and the Protestantism of the Protestant religion," who liked tea meetings and Bands of Hope and unctuous sermons, and who had a morbid hankering after marriage with his deceased wife's sister. Mr. Leslie Stephen has said:

"Condemned as he was to live and work among the middle class, while imbued with the ideas in which they were most defective, loving as he did the beauty and the fresh-

[1] *Essays in Criticism.*

ness of Oxford, the logical clearness and belief in ideas in France, the devotion to truth and philosophical thoroughness of Germany, the sight of the dogged British Philistine was to him a perpetual grievance."

Here is a passage from *Friendship's Garland* which tells its own story:

"What makes me look at France and the French with inexhaustible curiosity and indulgence is this: their faults are not of the same kind as ours, so we are not likely to catch them; their merits are not of the same kind as ours, so we are not likely to become idle and self-sufficient from studying them. I find such interest and instruction in considering a city so near London, and yet so unlike it. It is not that I so envy the Frenchman his café-haunting, domino-playing *bourgeois*. But when I go through Saint Pancras I like to compare our vestry-haunting, resolution-passing *bourgeois* with the Frenchman, and to say to myself, 'This, then, is what comes of not frequenting cafés nor playing dominoes! My countrymen here have got no cafés, and have never learnt dominoes, and see the mischief Satan has found for their idle hands to do!' Still I do not wish them to be the café-haunting, domino-playing Frenchmen, but rather some third thing, neither the Frenchmen nor their present selves."

No one who knows England well can deny that there is much truth in this kind of criticism. Matthew Arnold's diagnosis of some of our moral ailments was undoubtedly keen and just. But it was incomplete. He hardly ever did full justice to the many good and solid elements of national character which the English people owe to Puritanism. The case was in fact one of what Charles Lamb was wont to call "imperfect sympathies." Neither the British Philistine nor his critic ever fully understood or appreciated the other. Arnold, with his lofty air of distinction and his high-bred manners, sometimes appeared to those whom he criticised a rather dandified and supercilious cynic, going through the world as one who held a moral smelling-bottle at his nose, and exacting an impossible standard of life from a busy and strenuous people who had their living to get. And he, on the other hand, never ceased to call attention to their want of taste, their intellectual poverty, their great need of culture, of beauty, and "of sweetness and of light." This last phrase was seized upon by the public and often quoted as a proof of his superfine and unpractical ideals. When he went to receive the honorary degree of D.C.L. at Oxford, some wits suggested that Lord Salisbury, the Chancellor of the University, should address him *Vir dulcissime et lucidissime*. But beneath this famous and much criticised formula, Arnold had a real meaning and conviction, which was not without a serious significance for his countrymen.

It has been truly said that Arnold's criticisms did not manifest an adequate sense of what the religion of the English middle class had really been to it, what a source of vitality, energy, and persistent force. "*They who wait on the Lord*," says Isaiah, in words not less true than they are noble, "*shall renew their strength*," and the English middle class owes to its religion not only comfort in the past, but also a vast latent store of unworn life and strength for future progress. There was defective insight and some injustice in his failure to recognize this fact.

A closer study of history would probably have modified the contempt, half-amused and half-serious, with which Arnold regarded the English middle class. There was a time in the latter half of the seventeenth century when a great wave of irreligion and profligacy burst over English society, and, if we are to form our judgments solely from books of history, would appear to have well-nigh submerged all the best elements of the national character. But, after all, the vices of the Restoration period affected the Court and the upper ranks mainly; they touched the surface only of our social life. Down deeper lay the great solid mass of Puritan England, and in this the inbred probity, self-respect, and sense of righteousness remained for the most part uninfluenced by the wildness and licentiousness of the aristocracy. In like manner the eighteenth century saw in the Church of England decorum, learning, and many estimable qualities, but also coldness and a notable absence of religious fervour or of strong conviction. And it was to Wesley and Whitfield, and not to ecclesiastics in high places, that we owe the evangelical revival of that century. We have, as a nation, been in fact saved from moral corruption in the seventeenth century, and from religious apathy and indifference in the eighteenth, not by the influence of the educated and privileged classes, but by the great and stedfast qualities of that very class of British Philistines against whom

Matthew Arnold directed all his earnest condemnation and all the lighter artillery of his sarcasm and his wit.

There is another consideration which, in reading *Culture and Anarchy*, and books of the like kind, we are in some danger of overlooking. The Act of Uniformity of 1662, and the series of similar acts which constitute what is called the Clarendon Code, — Corporation Act, Test Act, Conventicle Act, and Five-Mile Act, — had been designed to stamp out Nonconformity and had made it a penal offence for a Dissenter either to preach in a chapel or to teach in any private or public school. For many years those who objected to sign the Articles and to conform to the worship of the Church of England were subject to heavy disabilities, as well as to irritating social exclusion. The Schism Act of 1713 enacted that "no person in Great Britain shall keep any public or private school, or act as tutor, that has not first subscribed the declaration to conform to the Church of England and obtained a licence from the diocesan, and that upon failure of so doing the party may be committed to prison without bail; and that no such licence shall be granted before the party produces a certificate of having received the sacrament according to the communion of the Church of England within the last year, and also subscribed the oaths of allegiance and supremacy." Until the year 1779 it continued to be illegal for a dissenter to act as a schoolmaster. The Test and Corporation Acts survived till the year 1829, and tests on admission to degrees in the Universities were not finally abolished by Parliament till 1871.

Thus it is scarcely just or generous on the part of churchmen, whose zeal for uniformity of belief has caused them during three centuries to exclude Dissenters from the Universities, from schools, from the higher professions, and from the public service, to reproach their fellow-countrymen with want of culture and with an ignoble ideal of education. If the English Nonconformist exhibited a watchful and habitual dread of State interference, it was because he and his ancestors had suffered much from such interference in days gone by. And if he was deficient in the graces, the accomplishments, and the tastes which are the products of a high and generous education, it ought at least to be remembered in his defence that the means of obtaining such education had been for many generations deliberately placed out of his reach. Probably if Arnold ever fully recognized the weight of these and the like considerations, some of his judgments would have been less severe, and he would have wounded and irritated the Nonconformists less.

That he was not insensible to the value of much of the work which they had done, or unmindful of the efforts they have made on behalf of education, many passages from his reports abundantly prove. Here is a sonnet which he wrote after meeting in the East End a well-known Congregational minister, the Rev. W. Tyler, whom as school manager and energetic worker in social improvement he had often encountered on his inspecting tours:

"'Twas August, and the fierce sun overhead
   Smote on the squalid streets of Bethnal Green,
   And the pale weaver, through his windows seen
   In Spitalfields, look'd thrice dispirited.

"I met a preacher there I knew, and said:
   'Ill and o'erwork'd, how fare you in this scene?'—
   'Bravely!' said he: 'for I of late have been
   Much cheer'd with thoughts of Christ, *the living bread.*'

"O human soul! as long as thou canst so
   Set up a mark of everlasting light,
   Above the howling senses' ebb and flow—
   To cheer thee, and to right thee if thou roam—
   Not with lost toil thou labourest through the night!
   Thou mak'st the heaven thou hop'st indeed thy home."

On his favourite theme, the need of a better system of secondary education, he wrote copiously. He thought the ideal prevalent among Englishmen of what a school ought to be and to do was often mean and ignoble. "I have this year," he says in a letter to me in 1880, "been reading *David Copperfield* for the first time. Mr. Creakle's school at Blackheath is the type of our ordinary middle-class schools, and our middle class is satisfied that so it should be."

And in another letter in 1881, referring to a project for a sort of trades' union among secondary and private teachers, designed partly for improving their own qualifications and status, but mainly for the protection of their professional interests, he tells me:

"I have seen the prospectus and will have nothing to do with it. It is just the sort of makeshift the English like, in order to escape a pressing necessity, such as the total reform of their middle class education. But a makeshift of this kind is not what is wanted. My whole use consists in standing out for the truth, the whole truth, and nothing but the truth, about our wretched middle class education and its needs."

By way of illustrating the difference between the position of a teacher responsible only to a recognized public body, and one whose sole business was to satisfy and to flatter ill-educated parents, he once wrote:

"The stamp of plainness and the freedom from charlatanism given to the instruction of our primary schools, through the public character which in the last thirty years it has received, and through its having been thus reserved, in great measure, from the influences of private speculation, is perhaps the best thing among them. It is in this respect that our primary schools compare so favourably with the private adventure schools of the middle class, that class which Mr. Bright says is perfectly competent to manage its own schools and education. The work in the one is appraised by impartial educated persons; in the other, by the common run of middle-class parents. To show the difference in the result, I will conclude by placing in juxtaposition a letter written in school by an ordinary scholar in a public elementary school in my district, a girl of eleven years old, with one written by a boy in a private middle-class school, and furnished to one of the Assistant-Commissioners of the Schools Inquiry Commission. The girl's letter I give first:

"'DEAR FANNY. — I am afraid I shall not pass in my examination; Miss C—— says she thinks I shall. I shall be glad when the Serpentine is frozen over, for we shall have such fun; I wish you did not live so far away, then you could come and share in the game. Father cannot spare Willie, so I have as much as I can do to teach him to cipher nicely. I am now sitting by the school fire, so I assure you I am very warm. Father and mother are very well. I hope to see you on Christmas Day. Winter is coming: don't it make you shiver to think of? Shall you ever come to smoky old London again? It is not so bad, after all, with its bustle and business and noise. If you see Ellen T—— will you kindly get her address for me? I must now conclude, as I am soon going to my reading class: so good bye.

"'From your affectionate friend

"'M.'

"And now I give the boy's:

"'MY DEAR PARENTS. — The anticipation of our Christmas vacation abounds in peculiar delights. Not only that its "festivities," its social gatherings and its lively amusements crown the old year with happiness and mirth, but that I come a guest commended to your hospitable love by the performance of all you bade me remember when I left you in the glad season of sun and flowers. And time has sped fleetly since reluctant my departing step crossed the threshold of that home whose indulgences and endearments their temporary loss has taught me to value more and more. Yet that restraint is salutary, and that self-reliance is as easily learnt as it is laudable, the propriety of my conduct and the readiness of my services shall ere long aptly illustrate. It is with confidence I promise that the close of every year shall find me advancing in your regard by constantly observing the precepts of my excellent tutors and the example of my excellent parents.

"'We break up on Thursday the 11th of December instant, and my impatience of the short delay will assure my dear parents of the filial sentiments of

"'Theirs very sincerely,

"'N.'

"'P. S. We shall reassemble on the 19th of January. Mr. and Mrs. P. present their respectful compliments.'

"To those who ask what is the difference between a public and a private school, I answer, *It is this.*"[1]

There was one class of English schools for which Arnold entertained a special dislike — schools erected by private, sectarian, or professional bodies for the separate instruction of their own children — *e.g.* schools for Clergy orphans, for sons of Freemasons, of Commercial Travellers, of officers in the Army, of Wesleyans, or of the Society of Friends. *Mutatis mutandis* these institutions were open to the same objections which apply to Poor Law schools, or to Ragged schools. They are filled in each case with scholars who have had the same antecedents and are drawn from the same class. Whatever disabilities attach to the class, whatever professional narrowness or prejudices belong to the homes from which they come, are intensified and rendered more mischievous by bringing the children together into an artificial community of this kind. What such children need most is the freer air, and the more varied conditions, which characterize a good school recruited from different classes of society. The happiest thing for a soldier's orphan, for example, is to be placed in a school with other children who are not orphans and whose fathers were not soldiers.

On this point Arnold spoke frequently and with much emphasis. For example, he thus contrasted the public character of some German middle schools under crown patronage, with the sectional and quasi-private establishments so common at home.

[1] Report to Education Department, 1867.

"But in England how different is the part which in this matter our governors are accustomed to play! The Licensed Victuallers or the Commercial Travellers propose to make a school for their children, and I suppose, in the matter of schools, one may call the Licensed Victuallers, or the Commercial Travellers, ordinary men, with their natural taste for the bathos still strong. And a sovereign with the advice of men like Wilhelm von Humboldt or Schleiermacher may, in this matter, be a better judge, and nearer to right reason. And it will be allowed, probably, that right reason would suggest that to have a sheer school of Licensed Victuallers' children, or a sheer school of Commercial Travellers' children, and to bring them all up, not only at home but at school too, in a kind of odour of licensed victualism or bagmanism, is not a wise training to give to these children. And in Germany, I have said, the action of the national guides or governors is to suggest and provide a better. But, in England, the action of the national guides or governors is, for a Royal Prince or a great minister to go down to the opening of the Licensed Victuallers' school, or of the Commercial Travellers' school, to take the chair, to extol the energy and self-reliance of the Licensed Victuallers or the Commercial Travellers, to be all of their way of thinking, to predict full success to their schools, and never so much as to hint to them that they are probably doing a very foolish thing, and that the right way to go to work with their children's education is quite different."[1]

[1] *Culture and Anarchy.*

Although, as we have seen, Arnold attached great value both to religion and poetry as factors in national education, there is one particular attempt to combine the two for which he had a curiously strong, but not unintelligible, aversion. He greatly disliked the ordinary hymns in use in our places of worship, and thought the national taste was degraded by the use we are accustomed to make of them.

"Our German kinsmen and we are the great people for hymns. The Germans are very proud of their hymns, and we are very proud of ours; but it is hard to say which of the two, the German hymn-book or ours, has least poetical worth in itself, or does least to prove genuine poetical power in the people producing it. . . . Only the German race, with its want of quick instinctive tact, of delicate, sure perception, could have invented the hymn as the Germans and we have it: and our non-German turn for style — style, of which the very essence is a certain happy fineness and truth of poetical perception — could not but desert us when our German nature carried us into a kind of composition which can please only when the perception is somewhat blunt. Scarcely any one of us ever judges our hymns fairly, because works of this kind have two sides — their side for religion and their side for poetry. Everything which has helped a man in his religious life, everything which associates itself in his mind with the growth of that life, is beautiful and venerable to him; in this way, productions of little or no poetical value, like the German hymns and ours, may come to be regarded as very precious. Their worth in this sense, as means by which we have been edified, I do not for a moment hold cheap; but there is an edification proper to all our stages of development, the highest as well as the lowest, and it is for man to press on towards the highest stages of his development, with the certainty that for those stages, too, means of education will not be found wanting. Now certainly it is a higher state of development when our poetical perception is keen than when it is blunt."[1]

And later he says with more decision:

"Hymns, such as we know them, are a sort of composition which I do not at all admire. I freely say so now, as I have often said it before. I regret their prevalence and popularity amongst us. Taking man in his totality and in the long run, bad music and bad poetry, to whatever good and useful purposes a man may often manage to turn them, are in themselves mischievous and deteriorating to him. Somewhere and somehow, and at some time or other, he has to pay a penalty and to suffer a loss for taking delight in them."

Dr. Johnson had in his life of Watts and elsewhere expressed the opinion that religious truths and worship were not the proper subjects for poetic treatment, and that all devotional poetry was for this reason more or less unsatisfactory. "The paucity of its topics enforces perpetual repetition, and the sanctity of the matter rejects the ornaments of figurative diction. It is sufficient for Watts to have done better than others what no man has done well."

Matthew Arnold, though not entirely for the same reason, disliked the current hymnology. He not only thought it contained bad poetry, but his fastidious literary taste and his sense of humour revolted against both its form and its substance. And in truth there is much in modern hymn-books to justify his criticism. In many hymns there is evident a painful attempt

[1] *Study of Celtic Literature.*

to pack as much theology as possible, rather than to raise religious emotion and to express devout aspiration. In many others the language put into the worshipper's mouth is sadly unreal and exaggerated, expressive of a warmth and rapture which is not likely to be actually felt, and which it is therefore confusing and benumbing to the possessor of a healthy conscience to pretend to feel. And a still larger number of hymns will be found to be disfigured by false metaphors, by prosaic and commonplace expressions, and by a complete absence of rhythm and poetry. Yet I think his rather indiscriminate and almost contemptuous judgment on religious poetry carried him too far. The Psalms of David, the mediæval Latin hymns, such as *O sol salutis* and the *Dies iræ*, the devotional poetry of Wither, of Herbert, of Milton, of Cowper, of Doddridge, of Charles Wesley, and of Keble, have in successive ages of the Church done too much in raising and ennobling the religious aspirations of men to be so summarily dismissed. Even John Henry Newman, long after his conversion to the Roman Church, thus commented on the influence of Keble's Christian Year:

"His poems became a sort of comment upon the formularies and ordinances of the Anglican Church, and almost elevated them into the dignity of a religious system. It kindled hearts towards his Church; it gave a something for the gentle and forlorn to cling to, and it raised up advocates for it among those who otherwise, if God and their good Angel had suffered it, might have wandered away into some sort of philosophy and acknowledged no Church at all."[1]

[1] Newman's *Essay Critical and Historical*, Vol. II., p. 441.

In fact, religious truth must ever be touched with emotion if it is to become a really vital force in the world, and when pure and unworldly strivings after a higher life are associated with musical words and a true poetic instinct, the hymn becomes a real factor in the religious life and education of the race. For example:

> "O God, our help in ages past,
> Our hope for years to come,
> Our shelter from the stormy blast,
> And our eternal home."

And these musical lines from the *Stabat Mater:*

> "Fac ut ardeat cor meum,
> In amando Christum Deum,
> Ut sibi complaceam."

But for all the intellectual and moral ailments which he observed and denounced in our social system, for the false taste, the bleakness, and the dulness of middle-class life, and for the absence of lofty ideals, he had, as is well known, one cure to urge. It was not a panacea. But it was the best and most potent, and at the same time the most readily available, corrective he knew. If our middle-class education was the worst in the world, if it lacked dignity, thoroughness, and refinement, the remedy was to ennoble our secondary schools, and the only possible instrument for effecting this object was the agency of the State. From his official inquiries in foreign countries he had, as we have seen, come back with no horror of bureaucracy or of a symmetrical system of public instruction. He thought that Englishmen had carried their love of freedom and of local and voluntary initiative in this matter too far, and that we were all suffering for it. He believed that the ideal of a good and generous education likely to be formed by responsible statesmen and enlightened administrators at headquarters was likely to prove in the long run higher and truer than that formed by vestries, town councils, sectarian committees, and local boards. The phantom of centralization did not frighten him, provided that State agency maintained a due regard to the genius, the feelings, the history and traditions and religious convictions, of the community. So in season and out of season, with a voice like that, as he was wont to confess, "of one crying in the wilderness," he constantly insisted on the need of attention to our great national defect. "*Porro unum est necessarium.* One thing is needful. Organize your secondary education."

The powers, he was fond of saying, which contribute to build up human civilization are the power of conduct, the power of intellect and knowledge, the power of beauty, the power of social life and manners. Expansion, conduct, science, beauty, manners,— here are the conditions of civilization, the claimants which man must satisfy before he can be humanized.

He was not sanguine about the immediate result of his preaching on this subject. In his well-known lecture, "*Ecce convertimur ad gentes,*" addressed to the members of a Workingmen's College, he says mournfully that "the one step towards that general improvement in our civilization which it is the object of all cultivating of our intelligence to bring about, the establishment of a genuine municipal system for the whole country, will hardly perhaps come in our time; men's minds have not yet been sufficiently turned to it for that." But subsequent events have shown that he undervalued the force and influence of his own crusade. In all later educational controversies, in Parliament, at the Universities, at Congresses, in meetings of teachers, and in the evidence and reports issued by Royal Commissions, his words have been constantly quoted, his facts referred to, and his authority invoked. Notably, the Report of the Royal Commission on Secondary Instruction, which was issued in 1895, proceeds to a large extent on lines which he was the first to trace, and recommends a policy which would have gone far to realize his hopes. And in the near future when English statesmen rouse themselves to a perception of the need of a coherent and well-ordered system of secondary schools, in which due regard shall be had not only to the claims of active life, but to the higher claims of the inner life for expansion and for purification, the result will be largely owing to the stimulus which his writings afforded and to the high and generous conception he had formed of the ends which ought to be attained in a liberal education, and of the spirit in which we ought to pursue them.

CHAPTER XII

Arnold as a literary critic, a humorist, and as a poet — Criticism and its functions — Comparison with Sainte Beuve — Examples of his critical judgments — Homer, Pope, and Dryden, Byron, Wordsworth, Burke, Tennyson, Charlotte Brontë, and Macaulay — The gift of humour indispensable to a critic — English newspapers — The *Telegraph* and the *Times* — His American experiences — His personal charm — Tributes of Mr. John Morley, Augustine Birrell, and William Watson — Poems — Arnold's place as a poet — Examples of his poems — General estimate of his own and his father's services to English education — Rugby Chapel

OUTSIDE the world of schools and Universities Matthew Arnold is better known, and is likely to be longer remembered, as a literary critic and as a poet, than as an official or as an advocate of improved public instruction. He was especially noticeable for the importance he attached to just criticism in relation to books and to life. He thought it the main function of a true critic first to know and then to set up a high standard of literary style and finish, and to judge all books by that standard. Criticism, he said, is the disinterested endeavour to learn and propagate the best that is known or thought in the world. It was the business of a critic to detect and to expose insincerity, vulgarity, the mere watchwords of parties and cliques, and in particular the slovenly and pretentious use of terms and phrases which were only half understood.

Arnold greatly valued and admired the influence

of the French Academy: "a sovereign organ of the highest literary opinion, a recognized authority in matters of intellectual tone and taste." Every one who knows what it is to take up a French book which has been *couronné* by the Academy, knows what this safeguard means. He thought that the corporation of forty of the most eminent French writers exercised great power in preserving the purity of their language, encouraging learning, and setting up before the whole nation a high ideal of beauty and perfection of style. Yet he doubted the wisdom of any attempt to introduce such an institution into England, and he thought our faults were not to be cured by that method.

"It is constantly said that I want to introduce here an institution like the French Academy. I have, indeed, expressly declared that I wanted no such thing. But let me notice how it is just our worship of machinery, and of external doing, which leads to this charge being brought; and how the inwardness of culture would make us seize, for watching and cure, the faults to which our want of an Academy inclines us, and yet prevent us from trusting to an arm of flesh — as the Puritans say; from blindly flying to this outward machinery of an Academy in order to help ourselves. . . . Every one who knows the characteristics of our national life, knows exactly what an English Academy would be like. We can see the happy family in one's mind's eye as distinctly as if it were already constituted. Lord Stanhope,[1] the Dean of St. Paul's,[2] the Bishop of Oxford,[3] Lord Houghton, Mr. Gladstone, the Dean of Westminster,[4] Mr. Froude,[5] Mr. Henry Reeve[6] — everything which is influ-

---

[1] The late Lord Stanhope.
[2] The late Dean Milman.
[3] The late Bishop Wilberforce.
[4] The late Dean Stanley.
[5] The historian.
[6] Late editor of the *Edinburgh Review*.

ential, accomplished, and distinguished; and then, some fine morning, a dissatisfaction of the public mind with this brilliant and select coterie, a flight of Corinthian leading articles, and an irruption of Mr. G. A. Sala. Clearly this is not what will do us good. The very same faults — the want of sensitiveness of intellectual conscience, the disbelief in right reason, the dislike of authority — which have hindered our having an Academy and have worked injuriously in our literature, would also hinder us from making our Academy, if we established it, one which would really correct them."[1]

But in the absence of any such recognized authority he regarded the function of the literary critic as one of high value. One of the most interesting acquaintances he ever made was that of Sainte Beuve, the accomplished author of the *Causeries de Lundi*, whose works he greatly admired and whom he met more than once in Paris. Of him he says in one of his letters: "Sainte Beuve gave me an excellent dinner and was in full vein of conversation, which as his conversation is about the best to be heard in France was charming. . . . I staid with him till midnight, and would not have missed my evening for the world. I think he likes me, and likes my caring so much about his criticisms and appreciating his extraordinary delicacy of tact and judgment in literature." Later, when Arnold contributed to the *Encyclopedia Britannica* a memoir of his friend, he used language which with little qualification might not inappropriately be applied to himself:

[1] *Culture and Anarchy*.

"He was a critic of measure, not exuberant, of the centre, not provincial, of keen industry and curiosity, with Truth (the word engraved in English on his seal) for his motto; moreover, with gay and amiable temper, his manner as good as his matter — the *'critique souriant,'* as in Monselet's dedication to him he is called. It so happens that the great place of France in the world is very much due to her eminent gift for social life and development, and this gift French literature has accompanied, fashioned, perfected, and continues to reflect. This gives a special interest to French literature, and an interest independent even of the excellence of individual French writers, high as that office is. And nowhere shall we find such interest more completely and charmingly brought out than in the *Causeries de Lundi* of this consummate critic. As a guide to bring us to a knowledge of the French genius and literature, he is unrivalled, perfect — so far as a poor mortal critic can be perfect — in judgment, in tact and tone." [1]

There was much in the serene intellectual detachment of Marcus Aurelius which to the last appealed powerfully to Arnold's sympathy. "We are all," says the Imperial Philosopher, "working together to one end, some with knowledge and design, and others without knowing what they do. But men co-operate after different fashions and even those co-operate abundantly who find fault with what happens and those who try to oppose it, and to hinder it; for the Universe hath need of such men as these." . . . "Reverence that which is best in the Universe, and in like manner reverence that which is best in thyself."

Herein we are reminded of the apostolic injunc-

[1] *Encyclopedia Britannica.*

tion: "Covet earnestly the *best* gifts!" This was the gist of Arnold's teaching in regard to literature. And he devoted much of his keen insight and fine and somewhat fastidious taste to the task of helping his countrymen to distinguish the good from the bad, the noble from the ignoble, the ephemeral from the enduring, in what they read. And if in doing this he made us profoundly dissatisfied with ourselves and with much of our current literature, he could not help it, and would not have helped it if he could. His lectures delivered at Oxford on *Translating Homer*, and his *Study of Celtic Literature*, are full of just and subtle criticism, and of comparisons between ancient and modern writing, which are not always flattering to ourselves, but are always worth remembering. For example, take these remarks on Homer and the grand style:

"The ballad-manner and the ballad-measure, whether in the hands of the old ballad poets, or arranged by Chapman or arranged by Mr. Newman, or even arranged by Sir Walter Scott, cannot worthily render Homer. And for one reason, Homer is plain, so are they; Homer is natural, so are they; Homer is spirited, so are they; but Homer is substantially noble, and they are not. Homer and they are both of them natural, and therefore touching and stirring; but the grand style which is Homer's is something more than touching and stirring; it can form the character; it is edifying. The old English balladist may stir Sir Philip Sidney's heart like a trumpet, and this is much; but Homer, like the few artists in the grand style, can do more; they can refine the raw natural man; they can transmute him. So it is not without cause that I say and say again to the translator of

Homer: never for a moment suffer yourself to forget our fundamental proposition, Homer is noble. For it is seen how large a share this nobleness has in producing that general effect of his, which it is the main business of a translator to *reproduce*."[1]

What, too, can be happier than some of his critical judgments? For example, this on Wordsworth and Byron: from his *Essays in Criticism*.

"Wordsworth has an insight into permanent sources of joy and consolation for mankind which Byron has not; his poetry gives us more which we may rest upon than Byron's — more which we can rest upon now, and which men may rest upon always. I place Wordsworth's poetry, therefore, above Byron's on the whole, although in some points he was greatly Byron's inferior, and although Byron's poetry will always, probably, find more readers than Wordsworth's, and will give pleasure more easily. But these two, Wordsworth and Byron, stand, it seems to me, first and pre-eminent in actual performance, a glorious pair, among the English poets of this century. Keats had probably, indeed, a more consummate poetic gift than either of them; but he died having produced too little, and being as yet too immature to rival them. I for my part can never even think of equalling with them any other of their contemporaries, — either Coleridge, poet and philosopher, wrecked in a mist of opium; or Shelley, beautiful and ineffectual angel, beating in the void his luminous wings in vain. Wordsworth and Byron stand out by themselves. When the year 1900 is turned, and our nation comes to recount her poetic glories in the century which has just ended, the first names will be these."

Dryden and Pope he regarded with admiration, but rather as skilful versifiers and the founders of classic

---

[1] On *Translating Homer*, Lecture II., p. 60.

prose than as inspired poets. He saw clearly their limitations when he came to compare them with Chaucer, with Milton, or with Wordsworth.

"We are to regard Dryden as the puissant and glorious founder, Pope as the splendid high priest, of our age of prose and reason, of our excellent and indispensable eighteenth century. For the purposes of their mission and destiny their poetry, like their prose, is admirable. Do you ask me whether Dryden's verse, take it almost where you will, is not good?

"'A milk-white Hind immortal and unchanged,
Fed on the lawns, and in the forest ranged.'

I answer: Admirable for the purposes of an inaugurator of an age of prose and reason. Do you ask me whether Pope's verse, take it almost where you will, is not good?

"'To Hounslow Heath, I point, and Banstead Down,
Thence comes your mutton, and these chicks my own.'

I answer: Admirable for the purposes of a high priest of an age of prose and reason. But do you ask me whether such verse proceeds from men with an adequate poetic criticism of life? from men whose criticism of life has a high seriousness, or, even without that high seriousness, has poetic largeness, freedom, insight, benignity? Do you ask me whether the application of ideas to life in the verse of these men, often a powerful application, no doubt, is a powerful *poetic* application? Do you ask me whether the poetry of these men has either the matter or the inseparable manner of such an adequate poetic criticism? whether it has the accent of

"'Absent thee from felicity awhile . . .'

or of

"'And what is else not to be overcome . . .'

or of

"'O martyr souded in virginitee!'

I answer: It has not, and can not have them; it is the poetry of the builders of an age of prose and reason. Though they may write in verse, though they may in a certain sense be masters of the art of versification, Dryden and Pope are not classics of our poetry: they are classics of our prose."

Of Gray, too, his appreciation is as guarded and careful as it is generous and just.

"Gray is our poetical classic of that literature and age. The position of Gray is singular and demands a word of notice here. He has not the volume or the power of poets who, coming in times more favourable, have attained to an independent criticism of life. But he lived with the great poets; he lived, above all, with the Greeks, though perpetually studying and enjoying them; and he caught their poetic point of view for regarding life, caught their poetic manner. The point of view and the manner are not self-sprung in him, he caught them of others, and he had not the free and abundant use of them. But whereas Addison and Pope never had the use of them, Gray had the use of them at times. He is the scantiest and frailest of classics in our poetry, but he is a classic."[1]

To another poet, Arthur Hugh Clough, whose early promise was never fully realized, but to whose genius Arnold's own was in many respects akin, he pays in *Thyrsis* an affectionate tribute, which after *Lycidas* is one of the noblest elegiac poems in our language. He also makes in one of his lectures a critical reference especially worth transcribing here, because it indicates his own exalted conception of the aims of the true poet.

[1] *Essays in Criticism*, Second Series.

"He possessed two invaluable literary qualities — a true sense for his object of study and a single-hearted care for it. He had both: but he had the second even more eminently than the first. He greatly developed the first through means of the second. In the study of art, poetry, or philosophy, he had the most undivided and disinterested love for his object in itself and the greatest aversion to mixing up with it anything accidental or personal. His interest was in literature itself, and it was this which gave so rare a stamp to his character, which kept him so free from all taint of littleness. In the saturnalia of ignoble personal passions, of which the struggle for literary success in old and crowded communities offers so sad a spectacle, he never mingled. He had not yet traduced his friends, nor flattered his enemies, nor disparaged what he admired, nor praised what he despised. Those who knew him well had the conviction that even with time, these literary arts would never be his. His poem has some admirable Homeric qualities — out of door freshness, life, naturalness, buoyant rapidity. Some of the expressions in that poem *Dangerous Corrievreckan* come back to my ear now with the true Homeric ring. But that in him of which I think oftenest is the Homeric simplicity of his literary life."

Arnold's estimate of Milton also is characterized by a generous appreciation and by keen critical discernment. For example:

"Milton's true distinction as a poet, for example, is undoubtedly his unfailing level of style. Milton has always the sure, strong touch of the master. His power both of diction and of rhythm is unsurpassable, and it is characterized by being always present — not depending on an access of emotion, not intermittent, but, like the pace of Raphael, working in its possessor as a constant gift of nature. . . . Shakespeare himself, divine as are his gifts, has not, of the marks of the master, this one — perfect sureness of hand in his style. Alone of English poets, alone of English art, Milton has it. He is our great artist in style, our one first-rate master in the grand style. He is as truly a master in this style as the great Greeks are, or Virgil, or Dante. The number of such masters is so limited that a man acquires a world rank in poetry and art, instead of a mere local rank, by being counted among them. But Milton's importance to us Englishmen, by virtue of this distinction of his, is incalculable. The charm of a master's unfailing touch in diction and in rhythm, no one, after all, can feel so intimately, so profoundly, as his own countrymen. Invention, plan, wit, pathos, thought — all of them are in great measure capable of being detached from the original work itself, and of being exported for admiration abroad: diction and rhythm are not."[1]

In a striking letter to M. Fontanès there is an incidental allusion to Burke, which will show how powerfully Arnold had been impressed with the grave wisdom, and yet with what appeared to him to be the somewhat limited foresight, of that statesman.

"Burke, like Wordsworth, is a great force in that epoch of concentration, as I call it, which arose in England in opposition to the epoch of expansion declaring itself in the French Revolution. The old order of things had not the virtue which Burke supposed. The Revolution had not the banefulness which he supposed. But neither was the Revolution the commencement, as its friends supposed, of a reign of justice and virtue. It was much rather, as Scherer has called it, 'un déchaînement d'instincts confus, un aveugle et immense besoin de renouvellement.' An epoch of concentration and of resistance to the crude and violent

[1] *Mixed Essays.*

people who were for imposing their 'renouvellement' on the rest of the world by force was natural and necessary. Burke is to be conceived as the great voice of this epoch. He carried his country with him, and was in some sort a providential person. But he did harm as well as good, for he made concentration too dominant an idea with us, and an idea of which the reign was unduly prolonged. The time for expansion must come, and Burke is of little help to us in presence of such a time. But in his sense of the crudity and tyranny of the French revolutionists, I do not think he was mistaken."[1]

Scattered up and down his writings and his familiar letters are many passages of this kind, showing a genuine and hearty appreciation of excellence in style or in thought. But the reader will often find to his surprise some outspoken dissent from the popular estimate even of the most admired of modern authors. For example, he never indulges in any raptures about Tennyson, the beauty and finish and the musical quality of whose verse did not reconcile Arnold to a certain thinness and want of force in his writings. "The fault I find with Tennyson in his *Idylls of the King*, is that the peculiar charm and aroma of the Middle Ages he does not give in them. . . . The real truth is that Tennyson, with all his temperament and artistic skill, is deficient in intellectual power, and no modern poet can make very much of his business unless he is pre-eminently strong in this."[2] Thackeray he did not regard as a great writer, and of Charlotte Brontë's *Villette* he

[1] Letters, Jan. 21, 1880.
[2] Letter, Dec. 17, 1860.

expressed himself with unwonted severity. "No fine writing can hide her faults. These will be fatal to her in the long run."[1]

And of Macaulay's style he says:

"Its external characteristic is a hard metallic movement, with nothing of the soft play of life, and its internal characteristic is a perpetual semblance of hitting the right nail on the head without the reality."[2]

"Macaulay's view of things is, on the whole, the view of them which the middle-class reader feels to be his own also. The persons and causes praised are those which he himself is disposed to admire; the persons and causes blamed are those with which he himself is out of sympathy. The rhetoric employed to praise or to blame them is animating and excellent. Macaulay is thus a great civilizer. In hundreds of men he hits their nascent taste for the things of the mind, possesses himself of it and stimulates it, draws it powerfully forth and confirms it. . . . At this stage rhetoric, even when it is so good as Macaulay's, dissatisfies. And the number of people who have reached this stage of mental growth is constantly, as things are now, increasing; increasing by the very same law of progress which plants the beginnings of mental life in more and more persons who, until now, have never known mental life at all. So that while the number of those who are delighted with rhetoric such as Macaulay's is always increasing, the number of those who are dissatisfied with it is always increasing too."[3]

On the whole it may be safely said that of all the literary critics of our time, none have done more than Arnold to purify the national taste, to help men in

---

[1] *Letter, April 19, 1853.* [2] *Friendship's Garland.* [3] *Mixed Essays.*

admiring what is admirable, and in eschewing what is tawdry and meretricious in literature. A sentence from the generous and affectionate estimate made by Mr. George Russell, in the charming little monograph which was privately printed in 1889, may be not improperly reproduced here, and will not by any real student of Arnold's writings be found to err by exaggeration or by a too indulgent memory.

"As a literary critic, his taste, his temper, his judgment were pretty nearly infallible. He combined a loyal and reasonable submission to literary authority with a free and even daring use of private judgment. His admiration for the acknowledged masters of human utterance — Homer, Sophocles, Shakespeare, Milton, Goethe — was genuine and enthusiastic, and incomparably better informed than that of some more conventional critics. Yet this cordial submission to recognized authority, this honest loyalty to established reputation, did not blind him to defects, did not seduce him into indiscriminate praise, did not deter him from exposing the tendency to verbiage in Burke and Jeremy Taylor, the excessive blankness of much of Wordsworth's blank verse, the undercurrent of mediocrity in Macaulay, the absurdities of Mr. Ruskin's etymology. And, as in great matters, so in small. Whatever literary production was brought under Matthew Arnold's notice, his judgment was clear, sympathetic, and independent. He had the readiest appreciation of true excellence, a quick eye for minor merits of facility and method, a severe intolerance of turgidity and inflation

— of what he called 'endeavours to render a platitude endurable by making it pompous,' and a lively horror of affectation and unreality. These, in literature as in life, were in his eyes the unpardonable sins."[1]

The gift of humour is a saving grace for its possessor, whatever his duties or pursuits may be. Even a lawyer, a clergyman, or a historian who possesses it is saved thereby from many mistakes and does his work the better for having it. To the literary critic it is indispensable. Without it, he is in constant danger of seeing things in false perspective and of failing to detect latent absurdities and to discriminate lesser from greater faults. It is not a gift which can be communicated, or can be secured by learning rules. It is certainly not a hereditary gift, for Arnold's father was curiously deficient in it. In the son it did not reveal itself in the form of merriment or fun, but rather in the keener perception of what was unreal, tawdry, or pretentious, in a genial sympathy, in general openness of mind, and in the capacity for seeing significant and insignificant details in their true proportion. A marked example of the use of this power is to be found in the prefaces to two little volumes of Extracts from the poems of Wordsworth and of Byron. He could not fail to perceive that the former had been led by his love of simplicity and his lack of humour to write much that was flat and commonplace, and that the poems of the latter were often disfigured by *banalités* unworthy of his genius. But he admired and appreciated both poets, and he sought

[1] Mr. G. W. E. Russell's "memorial sketch."

to pick out of their writings that work which was of finest quality and which best deserved to survive.

When rebuked by one of his critics for the light raillery and vivacity with which he often treated serious subjects, he replied: "We are none of us likely to be lively much longer. My vivacity is but the last sparkle of flame before we are all in the dark, the last glimpse of colour before we all go into the drab, the drab of the earnest, prosaic, practical, austerely literal future. Yes, the world will soon be the Philistines, and then with every voice not of thunder silenced, and the whole earth filled and ennobled every morning by the magnificent roaring of the young lions of the Daily Telegraph, we shall all yawn in one another's faces with the dismallest, the most unimpeachable gravity."[1]

After a discussion of the meaning of the *Zeitgeist*, and the tendencies of the modern movement, halting and uncertain as it is, towards perfection and a higher life, he thus speaks of England's favourite oracle, the *Times* newspaper:

"What is the 'Times'? — a gigantic Sancho Panza following by an attraction he cannot resist that poor, mad, scorned, suffering, sublime enthusiast, the modern spirit; following it, indeed, with constant grumbling, expostulation, and opposition, with airs of protection, of compassionate superiority, with an incessant by-play of nods, shrugs, and winks addressed to the spectators; following it, in short, with all the incurable recalcitrancy of a lower nature, but still following it."[2]

[1] *Essays in Criticism.*　　[2] *Friendship's Garland.*

Notable, too, is the delicate *persiflage* with which he referred to Frederick Maurice, for whom, nevertheless, he had a real admiration, as one who was "for ever beating the bush with profound emotion, but never starting the hare," and to some of the forms of what he called "pugilistic dissent," as exhibited in the arena of Birmingham. Even orthodox Churchmen were more amused than scandalized by the well-known sentences in which he summed up his investigation of the meaning and history of the three Christian creeds; "The Apostles' as popular science, the 'Nicene' as learned science, and the 'Athanasian' as learned science with a strong dash of temper in it."

Many of his severest judgments were passed upon contemporaries whose names have already faded into oblivion, but who seemed to him representatives of some passing and censurable phase of morals or politics. Though liberal in his convictions, he was not a party man, and his satire was directed impartially to the policy of both the great parties in the State; since both of them were liable, he thought, to be enslaved by claptrap or by the claims of faction. With him, it has been said, liberalism was not a creed, but a habit of mind. Some of the illustrations of modern liberalism and its tendencies which were afforded in the United States of America particularly interested him. His first impressions before visiting that country were gathered from books and newspapers alone, and were not favourable. He said: "Whereas our society in England distributes itself into Barbarians,

Philistines, and Populace, America is just ourselves, with the Barbarians quite left out, and the Populace nearly." To him, it thus seemed that the American community formed one gigantic middle class, with many of the faults which he had so often and so unmercifully exposed in the British Philistine. He said of the Americans that they were not an "interesting" people. And when, after much delay and hesitation, he determined to go on a lecturing tour in America, he said in a letter to me: "I don't like going. I don't like lecturing. I don't like living in public, and I wish it was well over. I shall be glad, however, to see an American common school with my own eyes." In fact, he saw much else besides common schools in his two visits to America. He was received with characteristic warmth and kindness by the leading men in the States; and like all others who have crossed the Atlantic and been admitted into the interior of many beautiful and delightful homes, his prejudices were greatly softened, and his admiration for the enterprise, the bright intelligence, the boundless faith in the future, and the splendour of the public institutions which characterized America and her people was greatly increased. *A Word more about America* and *Civilization in the United States*, and the volumes of *Discourses in America* will enable a reader to trace the gradual alteration which his actual transatlantic experience produced, and will account for the warmth with which he always acknowledged how much he had learned from his visits to the States.

Of the personal charm of his manner, of the air of distinction which always characterized him, and of the generosity of his nature, it is difficult to convey an adequate impression to those who did not know him intimately. Professor Max Müller has said of him: "He was beautiful as a young man, strong and manly, yet full of dreams and schemes. His Olympian manners began even at Oxford; there was no harm in them; they were natural, not put on. The very sound of his voice and the wave of his arm were Jove-like." At the Council Office, his colleagues were wont to look upon his visits as Adam and Eve regarded those of the "affable archangel" when he partook of their simple fare. He derived genuine pleasure from any favourable recognition of his literary work. If he thought it was good work, he would honestly admire it himself, and would not stoop to the affectation of pretending that it was a trifle, or of trying to extort a compliment from others by disparaging his own performance. "Have you read that article of mine in the *Contemporary?*" he would say. "Good, isn't it?" On one occasion I remember that there was an unusually savage and contemptuous article in the *Saturday Review* on a book he had just written. Meeting him a day or two later, he said to me: "Have you seen that article about my book?" I was unable to deny that I had read it, and simply replied that I had been sorry to read what was so unfair, and that I hoped it had not vexed him. "Why should it vex me?" he answered. "You see one's friends enjoy these things so much."

Mr. John Morley has on this point said with equal force and fairness: "It is true that Arnold talked, wrote, and thought much about himself, but not really much more than most other men and women who take their particular work and purpose in life seriously to heart. He was not the least of an egotist in the common ugly and odious sense of that terrible word. He was incapable of sacrificing the smallest interest of anybody to his own; he had not a spark of envy or jealousy; he stood well aloof from all the hustlings and jostlings by which selfish men push on; he bore life's disappointments — and he was disappointed in some reasonable hopes and anticipations — with good-nature and fortitude; he cast no burdens upon others, and never shrank from bearing his own share of the daily load, to the last ounce of it; he took the deepest, sincerest, and most active interest in the well-being of his country and his countrymen. Is it not absurd to think of such a man as an egotist, simply because he took a child's pleasure in his own performance and liked to know that somebody else thought well of his poetry, or praised his lecture, or laughed at his wit?"[1]

Mr. Augustine Birrell, in one of his clever and charming essays, shows a like generous and discriminating estimate of his friend's chief characteristics. "He was most distinctly on the side of human enjoyment. He conspired and contrived to make things pleasant. Pedantry he abhorred. He was a man of this life and this world. A severe critic of the world

[1] *Nineteenth Century*, December, 1895.

he indeed was, but finding himself in it, and not precisely knowing what is beyond it, like a brave and true-hearted man he set himself to make the best of it. Its sights and sounds were dear to him. The 'uncrumpling fern,' the 'eternal moon-lit snow,' 'Sweet William with its homely cottage-smell,' 'the red grouse springing at our sound,' the 'tinkling bells' of the 'high-pasturing kine,' the vagaries of men, women, and dogs, their odd ways and tricks, whether of mind or manner, all delighted, amused, tickled him. Human loves, joys, sorrows, human relationships, ordinary ties, interested him.

> "The help in strife,
> The thousand sweet still joys of such
> As hand in hand face earthly life."

"In a sense of the words which is noble and blessed, he was of the earth, earthy. . . . His mind was based on the plainest possible things. What he hated most was the fantastic,—the far-fetched, all elaborated fancies and strained interpretations. He stuck to the beaten track of human experience, and the broader the better. He was a plain-sailing man. This is his true note."[1]

Jowett, the Master of Balliol, who knew him well, said afterwards, "The world has been pleased to say many complimentary things of him since his death, but they have scarcely done him justice because they did not understand his serious side — hard work, in-

---

[1] *Res Judicatæ*, pp. 165–167.

dependence, and the most loving and careful fulfilment of all the duties of life." [1]

Another comment, that of a later poet, Mr. William Watson, is, though from a different point of view, worthy to be remembered:

> "It may be overmuch
> He shunned the common stain and smutch,
>   From soilure of ignoble touch
>   Too grandly free,
>   Too loftily secure in such
>   Cold purity.
> But he preserved from chance control
> The fortress of his stablished soul,
> In all things sought to see the Whole;
>   Brooked no disguise,
> And set his heart upon the goal,
>   Not on the prize." [2]

But, after all, Arnold's permanent fame will rest rather on his poems than on his prose writings. In the coming generations, when the educational politics of our day shall have become obsolete and have ceased to interest men; when the ephemeral literature, the sociology, and the personal controversies have passed out of view, his name will stand out conspicuously with those of Tennyson and Browning, the three representative poets of the latter half of the nineteenth century. The future historian of literature who seeks a key to the moral condition of the England of our time, to its intellectual unrest, and to its spiritual

---

[1] *Life of Benjamin Jowett*, Vol. II., p. 338.
[2] *In Laleham Churchyard.*

aims and tendencies, will find it here. Matthew Arnold will never be a popular poet in the ordinary sense of the term. He has not the smoothness, the finish, and the music of Tennyson, and does not choose for the subjects of his verse familiar and superficially attractive topics. Some of his best work, such as the *Strayed Reveller* and *Empedocles on Etna* and *Dejaneira*, presupposes a more or less scholarly acquaintance with classical forms and modes of thought on the part of the reader, and carries him into a region remote from modern life and associations. To many of his metres, too, the ear of the average reader is not yet attuned. In fact, he does not specially challenge the attention of average readers at all. His ear was often at fault; a few of his lines are not easy to read aloud or to scan. And even in poems which are full of beauty and of noble emotion, one is sometimes irritated by such cacophony as occurs in the final line of the sonnet already quoted:

"Thou mak'st the heaven thou hop'st indeed thy home."[1]

Moreover, his poems are for the most part overcast with thought which at least is serious and not often exhilarating. He was wont to say that for the higher purpose of literature the people required joy. But his own muse was somewhat sombre and introspective, and he was heavily weighted with a sense of the mystery and gloom and disappointment of human life. The vastness and intricacy of the problems which yet remain unsolved, and our inability to solve

[1] *Supra*, p. 230.

them, sometimes oppressed him. Of England and her destiny he said:

> " The weary Titan with deaf
> Ears and labour-dimmed eyes,
> Regarding neither to right
> Nor left, goes passively by
> Staggering on to her goal;
> Bearing on shoulders immense,
> Atlanteän, the load
> Well-nigh not to be borne,
> Of the too vast orb of her fate." [1]

Readers of *In Memoriam* and of *Christmas Eve* and *Easter Day* will be reminded, as they take up Arnold's poems, of the fact that all three — Tennyson, Browning, and Arnold — had been greatly influenced by the modern critical spirit in relation to many venerable and consecrated beliefs. Yet these writers did not approach modern thought and speculation in the same spirit. There is in Arnold little of the rather helpless lament over an unforgotten but irrecoverable belief, such as is to be found in *In Memoriam*, where weak faith is seen trying to come to the aid of weak doubt; but a sane and manly recognition of the truth that while some changes in the form of men's religious life are inevitable, the spirit and the power of the Christian faith are sure to survive. Nor does Arnold express often the strong scorn for some of the conventional beliefs which shows itself not less in the exasperating ruggedness of Browning's verse than in the less serious scepticism of Shelley's *Queen*

[1] *Heine's Grave.*

Mab. In such poems as *Obermann* and *Stanzas from the Grand Chartreuse* we have evidence of Arnold's oppressive sense of the burden of life, and of the need of restfulness, affection, and calm.

> "Awhile let me with thought have done,
> And as this brimm'd unwrinkled Rhine,
> And that far purple mountain-line,
> Lie sweetly in the look divine
> Of the slow-sinking sun:
>
> "So let me lie, and, calm as they,
> Let beam upon my inward view
> Those eyes of deep, soft, lucent hue —
> Eyes too expressive to be blue,
> Too lovely to be grey.
>
> "Ah! Quiet, all things feel thy balm!
> Those blue hills too, this river's flow,
> Were restless once, but long ago.
> Tamed is their turbulent youthful glow;
> Their joy is in their calm."[1]

His appreciation of Wordsworth was not confined to such criticism as we have already quoted, but expressed itself gracefully in verse.

> "Raised are the dripping oars,
> Silent the boat! — the lake,
> Lovely and soft as a dream,
> Swims in the sheen of the moon.
> The mountains stand at its head
> Clear in the pure June night,
> But the valleys are flooded with haze.
> Rydal and Fairfield are there;

[1] *On the Rhine.*

In the shadow Wordsworth lies dead.
So it is, so it will be for aye.
Nature is fresh as of old,
Is lovely; a mortal is dead.

"The spots which recall him survive,
For he lent a new life to these hills.
The Pillar still broods o'er the fields
Which border Ennerdale Lake,
And Egremont sleeps by the sea.
The gleam of The Evening Star
Twinkles on Grasmere no more,
But ruin'd and solemn and grey
The sheepfold of Michael survives;
And, far to the south, the heath
Still blows in the Quantock coombs,
By the favourite waters of Ruth.
These survive — yet not without pain,
Pain and dejection to-night,
Can I feel that their poet is gone.

*   *   *   *   *

"Well may we mourn when the head
Of a sacred poet lies low
In an age which can rear them no more!
The complaining millions of men
Darken in labour and pain;
But he was a priest to us all
Of the wonder and bloom of the world,
Which we saw with his eyes, and were glad.
He is dead, and the fruit-bearing day
Of his race is past on the earth;
And darkness returns to our eyes."[1]

That he had caught the spirit of Wordsworth is manifest in many of his poems. The experiences of

[1] *The Youth of Nature.*

a starry night, his solemn musings on the magnitude and richness of the visible world, had a tranquillizing effect upon him. For example:

> "'Ah, once more,' I cried, 'ye stars, ye waters,
> On my heart your mighty charm renew;
> Still, still let me, as I gaze upon you
> Feel my soul becoming vast like you!'

> "From the intense, clear, star-sown vault of heaven,
> Over the lit sea's unquiet way,
> In the rustling night air came the answer:
> 'Would'st thou *be* as these are? *Live* as they.'

> "Unaffrighted by the silence round them,
> Undistracted by the sights they see,
> These demand not that the things without them
> Yield them love, amusement, sympathy.

> "And with joy the stars perform their shining,
> And the sea its long moon-silver'd roll:
> For self poised they live, nor pine with noting
> All the fever of some differing soul.

> "Bounded by themselves, and unregardful
> In what state God's other works may be,
> In their own tasks all their powers pouring,
> These attain the mighty life you see."

> "O air-born voice! long since, severely clear,
> A cry like thine in mine own heart I hear;
> 'Resolve to be thyself, and know that he
> Who finds himself, loses his misery!'"[1]

Examples of his narrative power are best shown in his story of *Sohrab and Rustum* and in *Tristram and*

[1] *Self-dependence.*

Iseult. His lyric poems, notably *Philomela* and the *Fragment of an 'Antigone,'* show how thoroughly saturated his mind was with Greek thought and traditions, and how admirably he could unite the sensibility and intellectual experience of a modern Englishman with the luminousness and simplicity which characterized the forms of Greek poesy. His *Merope* is, with the possible exception of Mr. Swinburne's *Atalanta in Calydon,* the best reproduction since *Samson Agonistes* of both the spirit and the form of the Greek tragedy, its ethical purpose, its massive dignity, and the solemn, overhanging sense of the greatness of man's destiny, whether seen in warring against adverse circumstances, or even in being subdued by them.

One extract more will serve to illustrate his descriptive power. It was suggested by his visit to the great Carthusian monastery in Switzerland.

STANZAS FROM THE GRANDE CHARTREUSE

The silent courts where night and day
Into their stone-carved basins cold
The splashing icy fountains play;
The humid corridors behold!
Where, ghostlike in the deepening night,
Cowl'd forms brush by in gleaming white.

The chapel where no organ's peal
Invests the stern and naked prayer —
With penitential cries they kneel
And wrestle; rising then, with bare
And white uplifted faces stand,
Passing the Host from hand to hand;

Each takes, and then his visage wan
Is buried in his cowl once more.
The cells! — the suffering Son of Man
Upon the wall! — the knee-worn floor —
And where they sleep, that wooden bed,
Which shall their coffin be when dead!

The library where tract and tome
Not to feed priestly pride are there,
To hymn the conquering march of Rome,
Nor yet to amuse, as ours are!
They paint of souls the inner strife,
Their drops of blood, their death in life.

The garden overgrown — yet mild;
See, fragrant herbs are flowering there!
Strong children of the Alpine wild
Whose culture is the brethren's care;
Of human tasks their only one,
And cheerful works beneath the sun.

No just estimate of Matthew Arnold's influence on English education is possible without taking into due account his position and work in the outside world, and especially in the world of letters. He himself would have been the first to admit that public education, important as it is, was only one of the interests, and not the paramount interest of his life. Yet it is surely not a small episode in the history of education in England that for thirty years, one of the chief administrative offices in the Bureau of public instruction should have been filled by one of her most illustrious poets. Unconsciously and indirectly his influence over his colleagues, over the teachers, and over the children was all the greater because he was a poet; for he saw them all with the clear and penetrating eye of genius and not with that of a pedant or a merely industrious official. For example, some readers of his latest foreign report were a little puzzled to interpret a sentence in which he said of some German schools, "Again and again I find written in my notes, *The children are human.*" It is not of course to be supposed that he meant to imply that in English schools the children were not human; but only that speaking as a poet, he recognized in some German schools the presence of other influences than those of ordinary lessons, the freedom and the naturalness which can come only from a true sympathy between teacher and taught.

He rests in the quiet graveyard of Laleham, close to his early home, side by side with his three sons, Thomas, Basil, and Trevenen, and a little grandchild. Over him is the inscription: —

There is sprung up a light for the righteous and joyful gladness for such as are true-hearted.

Thus it has been attempted to show that Thomas and Matthew Arnold, father and son, have both played a conspicuous and influential part in the improvement of English education and in the shaping of English thought. They did this in different ways. They approached the educational problem from very different points of view. One saw it with the eyes of a poet and a philosopher, the other with those of an earnest Christian teacher and moralist. But they were alike in many respects. To both the formation of character was an object of more importance than the acquisition of knowledge. To both it seemed that "conduct was three-fourths of life." Both were disposed to measure a man or boy rather by what he *is* than by what he believes and knows. Both believed in the supreme importance of letters, language, and the discipline of thought as the instruments for attaining the desired end. Both attached high value to religious and moral training; but neither identified that training with the enforcement of human formularies and creeds. To both it seemed that reverence for the past and a sympathetic acquaintance with the best that has been written and thought in the world constituted the most valuable preparation a scholar could have for his present duties and for his future development. To both the attainments which helped a man to live a noble and intelligent life were of higher value than those which helped him to 'get a living,' however successfully. Both tried to emancipate themselves from whatever hindrances conventional and traditional modes of thinking placed in the way of a fearless pursuit of truth.

It must be owned that both set before themselves a higher ideal than any we have yet attained, and that we are following after it with halting and feeble steps. But if either now or in the days to come our great public schools assume a higher tone, and our whole system of national instruction is organized on a noble and enduring basis; if commercial prosperity is no longer held by any of us to satisfy the claims of the spiritual and social life; if the standard of literary excellence becomes more exalted and more pure; and if the splendid triumphs of physical science do not succeed in beguiling us into a neglect of the older and humaner studies,—the future historian will be able to attribute these results in large measure to the influence of the two Arnolds. For each of them in his own way sought to illuminate the conscience of his fellow-countrymen, to make them profoundly discontented with what was mediocre and unreal in their lives and in their literature, and to enlarge their conception of a liberal education so that it should include not book-learning only, but "whatsoever things are true, whatsoever things are honest, what soever things are just, whatsoever things are pure, whatsoever things are lovely and whatsoever things are of good report."

The characters of both men are well revealed in these extracts from a memorable poem which the son wrote in November, 1867, on visiting the scene of his father's work.

RUGBY CHAPEL

O strong soul, by what shore
Tarriest thou now? For that force,
Surely, has not been left vain!
Somewhere, surely, afar,
In the sounding labour-house vast
Of being, is practised that strength,
Zealous, beneficent, firm!

Yes, in some far-shining sphere,
Conscious or not of the past,
Still thou performest the word
Of the Spirit in whom thou dost live —
Prompt, unwearied, as here!
Still thou upraisest with zeal
The humble good from the ground.
Sternly repressest the bad!
Still, like a trumpet, dost rouse
Those who with half-open eyes
Tread the border-land dim
'Twixt vice and virtue; reviv'st,
Succourest! — this was thy work,
This was thy life upon earth.

* * * *

If, in the paths of the world,
Stones might have wounded thy feet,
Toil or dejection have tried
Thy spirit, of that we saw
Nothing — to us thou wast still
Cheerful, and helpful, and firm!
Therefore to thee it was given
Many to save with thyself;
And, at the end of thy day,
O faithful shepherd! to come,
Bringing thy sheep in thy hand.

And through thee I believe
In the noble and great who are gone;
Pure souls honour'd and blest
By former ages, who else —
Such, so soulless, so poor,
Is the race of men whom I see —
Seem'd but a dream of the heart,
Seem'd but a cry of desire.
Yes! I believe that there lived

Others like thee in the past,
Not like the men in the crowd
Who all round me to-day
Bluster or cringe, and make life
Hideous, and arid, and vile;
But souls temper'd with fire,
Fervent, heroic, and good,
Helpers and friends of mankind.

Servants of God! or sons,
Shall I not call you? because
Not as servants ye knew
Your Father's innermost mind,
His, who unwillingly sees
One of his little ones lost —
Yours is the praise, if mankind
Hath not as yet in its march
Fainted, and fallen, and died!

See! In the rocks of the world
Marches the host of mankind,
A feeble, wavering line.
Where are they tending? A God
Marshall'd them, gave them their goal.
Ah! but the way is so long!
Years they have been in the wild!
Sore thirst plagues them, the rocks,
Rising all round, overawe;
Factions divide them, their host
Threatens to break, to dissolve.
— Ah, keep, keep them combined!
Else, of the myriads who fill
That army, not one shall arrive;
Sole they shall stray; in the rocks
Stagger for ever in vain,
Die one by one in the waste.

Then, in such hour of need
Of your fainting, dispirited race,
Ye, like angels, appear,
Radiant with ardour divine!
Beacons of hope, ye appear!
Languor is not in your heart,
Weakness is not in your word,
Weariness not on your brow.
Ye alight in our van! at your voice
Panic, despair flee away.
Ye move through the ranks, recall
The stragglers, refresh the outworn,
Praise, re-inspire the brave!
Order, courage, return.
Eyes rekindling, and prayers,
Follow your steps as you go.
Ye fill up the gaps in our files,
Strengthen the wavering line,
Stablish, continue our march,
On, to the bound of the waste,
On, to the City of God.

INDEX

Academy, the French, 242.
America, 257.
American secular schools, 210.
Aristotle, 7, 35, 103.
Arnold, Matthew, his estimate of his father, 150; his life and letters, 158; his appointment to an inspectorship, 159; his letters, 160; his work as inspector, 167; his foreign journeys, 200; his reports, 210; his literary criticisms, 241; his poems, 250.
Arnold, Thomas, his parentage and early life, 3; school, 4, 9; the University, 4, 11, 15, 16; Laleham, 18; his aims and studies, 19; election to Rugby, 22; his scheme of school work, 33; his relation to his staff, 71; his preaching, 84; his favourite pursuits, 110; his delight in nature, 113; Oxford controversies, 138; lectures, 148; death, 149.
Ascham, 30.
Assistant masters, 69.
Athletics, 103.

Bacon, 45, 49, 52.
Barbarians, the, 221.
Biblical teaching in the common school, 194.
Biography, 2, 59.
Birkbeck, Dr., 125.
Birrell, Mr. Augustine, quoted, 259.
Bowyer, 46.
Boyle, Dean, quoted, 153, 167.
Bradley, Dean, 155.
British history, early, 63.
Brontë, Charlotte, 251.

Brown's, Tom, School Days, 104.
Brougham, Lord, 124, 126.
Browning, 6.
Browning, Mr. Oscar, quoted, 66, 103.
Buckland, Mr., of Laleham, 18.
Burke, 250.
Busby, 30.
Butler, Bishop, 12.
Byron, 246.

Campbell, Thomas, and the London University, 126.
Carlyle, 2, 66, 107.
Christian Knowledge Society, 130.
Church, Dean, 136, 142, 147.
Cicero, 46, 65.
Civil service examinations, 207.
Classical studies vindicated, 35.
Clerical schoolmasters, 97.
Clough, A. H., 83, 248.
Coleridge, Mr. Justice, 8, 10.
Coleridge, S. T., 6, 7, 46, 55, 141, 246.
Colet, Dean, 26.
Comenius, 30.
Competitive examinations, 218.
Composition exercises, 38.
Construing, 43.
Continental schools, 213.
Copleston, 16.
Cowardice, 87.
Cowper, 6.
Crabbe, 6.
Criticism and its functions, 242.

Darwin, 52.
Davison, 16.
Delafield, Miss, 3.
Democracy, 203.
Demosthenes, 45, 46.
De Tocqueville, 202.

Diffusion of Useful Knowledge, The Society for, 125, 128, 130.
Dryden, 6, 246.

Edinburgh Review, 72, 148.
Endowments, in France, 215.
English literature studies, 46.
Englishman's Register, the, 122.
English society, 221.
Erasmus, 25, 142.
Eton, A French, 208, 211.
Examinations, 217.
Expulsion, 83.

Farrar, Dean, on Greek and Latin versification, 39.
Foreign schools, 201.
Foreign travel, 111.
Formative studies, 183.
Forster, Mr. W. E., 153.
France, 205.
Fuller quoted, 72.

Gabell, Dr., of Winchester, 10.
Geography, its bearing on history, 67.
Germany, 204.
Goddard, Dr., of Winchester, 10.
Governing bodies, 73.
Grammar in the elementary school, 185.
Gray, 248.
Griffiths, Dr., of Warminster, 9.
Grindal, Archbishop, founder of St. Bees, 28.
Grote, George, quoted, 104.
Guizot as education minister, 209.

Hampden, R. D., Bishop of Hereford, 16, 136.
Hawkins, Dr., 16, 22.
Healing, Mr., quoted, 173.
Heine, 205.
Herodotus, 7, 45, 67.
History, the teaching of, 54, 64.
Holland, 214.
Home discipline, 117.
Homer, 46, 245.

Hooker, 12, 45, 143.
Horace, 65.
Howe, Lord, 73.
Howson, Dean, of Chester, 154.
Hughes, Thomas, quoted, 26, 41, 82.
Humour, 254.
Huxley, 52, 187.
Hymns, 235.

Inspector, the office of, 168, 182.
Intellectual cultivation a religious duty, 89.
Isaiah as a school-book, 195.

Jowett, 143, 155, 260.
Juvenal, 65.

Kay Shuttleworth, 152.
Keble, John, 16, 21, 23, 237.
Knight, Charles, 125.

Laleham, 17.
Latin in the elementary school, 186.
Laurie, Professor, quoted, 60.
Learning by heart, 183.
Livy, 7, 65.
Locke, 30.
Lockyer, 52.
London University, 126, 131.
Louis, St., of France, 65.
Luther, 142.

Macaulay, 252.
Marcus Aurelius, 244.
Mechanics' Institute, 121, 125, 131.
Memory exercises, 185.
Milton, 249; his educational theories, 30.
Moberly, Dr., 76, 154, 158.
Modern and ancient history, 57.
Montaigne, quoted, 11.
Moral evils in schools, 77.
Morley, Mr. John, quoted, 259.
Mozley, J. B., quoted, 139.

INDEX

Napoleon, 65, 67.
Naturkunde, 187.
Nelson, 5.
Newman, J. H., 136, 237.
Niebuhr, 19, 62, 67.
Nonconformists, 224.

Oriel, Fellows of, 15, 16.
Oxford, 7, 16.
Oxford Malignants, the, 138.
Oxford movement, the, 135.

Paley's evidences, 12.
Paul's, St., School, statutes, 29.
Pedagogy, 191.
Percival, Bishop, quoted, 108.
Pestalozzi, 30.
Philistines, the, 223.
Poetry, learning of, 185.
Politics, 121.
Polybius, 65, 66.
Poor, intercourse with the, 119.
Pope, 6.
Price, Mr. Bonamy, 17.
Professorship of modern history, 147.
Public and private schools, 8, 93, 231.
Punishments, 101.
Puritanism, 225.
Pusey, E. B., 135.

Religious teaching, 84.
Roman history, 63.
Rousseau, 30.
Rugby Chapel, 271.
Rugby School, Arnold's appointment to the, 22; mastership, 22; its history, 25.
Russell, Mr. G. E., quoted, 253.

Sainte-Beuve, 243.
Schools, endowed grammar, 25.
Science, physical, its educational claims, 52.
Scott, Sir W., 6.
Scripture at the London University, 133.

Sermons, 84.
Shakespeare, 46.
Sheffield Courant, the, 123.
Sheriff, Lawrence, founder of Rugby School, 25.
Socratic questioning, 50.
Sorèze, the school at, 212.
Southey, 6.
Spencer, Herbert, 53.
Stanley, Bishop, 142.
Stanley, Dean, as a biographer, 2; as a school-boy, 32, 62.
Storr, Mr. Francis, quoted, 48.
Sunday services and studies, 21.
Switzerland and its schools, 214.

Tacitus, 35, 56.
Taylor, Jeremy, 12.
Tennyson, 6, 12, 251, 263.
Thring, Edward, quoted, 47.
Thucydides, 7, 55.
Times, the newspaper, 255; tribute to Arnold's memory, 155.
Toulouse, the Lyceum at, 211.
Tracts for the *Times*, 136, 145.
Traditions, school, 94.
Trafalgar, 5.
Translation v. Construing, 44.

Unsectarian religious teaching, 194.

Vacation reading parties, 118.
Versification, 39.

Welldon, Mr. J. E. C., quoted, 79.
Whateley, Archbishop, 16.
Wight, Isle of, Arnold's early home, 5.
Winchester, 9.
Wooll, Dr., of Rugby, 21, 26.
Worboise, Miss E. J., 3.
Wordsworth, 6, 246.
Wykeham and Wykehamists, 9.

Xenophon, 7.

www.ingramcontent.com/pod-product-compliance
Lightning Source LLC
Chambersburg PA
CBHW032107230426
43672CB00009B/1663